GAMEBIRD TAXIDERMY
with Frank Newmyer

Gamebird Taxidermy

with

Frank Newmyer

Roger Schroeder

and

Frank Newmyer

Stackpole Books

Published by
STACKPOLE BOOKS
Cameron and Kelker Streets
P.O. Box 1831
Harrisburg, PA 17105

First Edition

Printed in the U.S.A.

Library of Congress Cataloging-in-Publication Data

Schroeder, Roger, 1945–
    Gamebird taxidermy with Frank Newmyer / Roger Schroeder and Frank
Newmyer. – 1st ed.
        p.   cm.
    Bibliography: p.
    ISBN 0-8117-0701-6
    1. Taxidermy. 2. Game and game-birds.   I. Newmyer, Frank.
II. Title.
QL63.S37 1989
579′.4 – dc20

Contents

Acknowledgments

Those who have contributed to the making of this book are Robert Perrish, William Brandenburg, Pat Godin, Howard Nixon, and Judith Schnell. Our thanks go out to them.

Introduction

It is safe to say that the first traces of modern taxidermy date back to less than five hundred years ago. Yet taxidermy as the sophisticated art form it is today is less than a decade old.

If taxidermy has any antecedents, they are to be found in animal preservation. We know that embalmed specimens of cats, monkeys, ibises, and other animals, as well as humans, were put into Egyptian tombs. This practice dates back some four thousand years. Nearly fifteen hundred years later, a Carthaginian navigator named Hanno described the capture of gorillas. Once killed, their skins were taken to Carthage and put on display.

But taxidermy as we know it today attempts to put specimens into some lifelike pose, not merely preserve their skins. We must look another two thousand years to find the first mention of taxidermy: in Amsterdam in the sixteenth century. There skins were arranged on wires, and spices were employed to preserve them, apparently for sportsmen who wanted their hunting trophies saved. Shakespeare, in *Romeo and Juliet*, dated 1599, makes mention of an apothecary shop in which were hung a stuffed alligator, skins, and "ill-shap'd fishes." The description strongly suggests that taxidermy of the late 1500s still had far to go in making specimens look true to their nature.

What, then, does the word "taxidermy" mean? Simply, it derives from two Greek words. "Taxis" means arrange and "derma" means skin. What we have is a definition that describes the methods of removing the skin of an animal and preserving it on a form.

In the late seventeenth century the first publication on the art of taxidermy appeared. By this time chemicals for preserving hair, feathers, and skin had been developed to some degree. More texts came into print in the eighteenth and nineteenth centuries, and the first U.S. publication appeared the year the Civil War ended.

Over the last century the basic techniques of taxidermy have not changed much, though the chemicals and materials have. Traditionally, the skin is removed from the animal by making an incision along the

World Champion Frank Newmyer displays his taxidermy awards, trophies, and ribbons.

stomach. The skin is then pickled in a solution of salt, a compound called alum, and water. Later it is rinsed, and the hair or feathers are dried in warm sand or sawdust. Next the head, legs, and tail are wired. These wires are twisted together inside the body cavity. The body is filled with a material like straw, grass or, more recently, excelsior or wood wool. The skin is then sewn together, and the animal is put on its feet and mounted with the wires that protrude through them.

My earliest introduction to taxidermy was seeing a deer head mounted over my grandfather's fireplace. I will always remember how lifelike it looked despite its disembodied head and glass eyes. Perhaps it helped to shape my own interest in mammals and later in birds.

But my most profound awareness of taxidermy came with my early visits to the Museum of Natural History, located in New York City. I was preoccupied with the dinosaur bones, for I wanted to be an archaeologist. But I was also enthralled with the amazing dioramas of African velds and savannas, of South American rain forests and Asian habitats. Each scene was filled with animals and plants indigenous to that environment.

I was to learn later that the finest examples of taxidermy work could be found in this country. One of the best taxidermists was Carl Akeley (1864–1926), who developed techniques for sculpturing bodies in clay and plaster and mounting skins on them. For Akeley and others doing museum mounting, anatomically correct mannikins became essential to good taxidermy.

For most of the last century, however, good taxidermy could rarely be found outside of museums, and the science seemed to be dominated by those deer heads that found their way into so many American homes. The only other taxidermy work I recall from when I was growing up were awkward-looking birds stiffly wired to boards, their feathers so faded that their species were hard to identify.

It is with this history in mind that I introduce you to an exceptional taxidermist: Frank Newmyer. His specialty is birds, gamebirds in particular. His wildfowl are portrayed in poses that best highlight individual characteristics of the species, and many of them are arranged in minihabitats not unlike those I viewed in the Museum of Natural History. Among his works can be found a drumming grouse standing erect, its wings seemingly fanning the air in front of it. Its habitat includes mushrooms, grass, leaves—virtually a piece of the woods—all fashioned from artificial and inorganic materials. The display is presented on a wooden base that is enclosed with glass.

Still other ducks mounted by Frank swim on resinous water. Rocks are made from rigid foam, and reeds are shaped from paper or metal, all painted with such accuracy that the viewer cannot discern their origins.

But Frank has gone beyond putting taxidermic birds into watery habitat. Some of his gamebirds actually seem to fly, or at least they are credibly suspended in air with inconspicuous supports. One such piece portrays a flushing duck rising from "water," or resin, with droplets of the resin streaming from its feathers.

Newmyer has introduced an artistic way to bring natural history out of the museum and into homes and workplaces. With his amazing eye for design and composition, he has been able to put birds into natural-looking habitats, some even small enough to be put on a table or desk. As Joe Kish, editor of *Taxidermy Review,* put it, Frank has led in elevating taxidermy from a craft to a fine art. Kish adds that Newmyer's style of animated poses and inorganic habitat is being imitated by a great number of people. It is no wonder that another writer described him as the Picasso of taxidermy.

Taxidermy has experienced an explosion of interest in the past decade, and much of that interest has been due to Frank's efforts. As far back as 1978, Frank was writing articles in national magazines about anatomy and habitat. And he has displayed his work at art shows and exhibits around the country.

As the number of taxidermists has increased during

the last decade, so have the competitions, which have forced taxidermists to push their work to the limits of pose, design, and composition.

Awards with names like the Gold Medallion and World Champion and People's Choice have come into being. And Frank has won them all. In fact, he has won more Gold Medallions, more best in shows, more People's Choices, and more blue ribbons than any other taxidermist in the world. With ninety-two entries in fifteen major shows over a span of only six years, Frank has achieved an incredible array of winnings. In 1983 the World Taxidermy Championships held the first Carl Akeley Invitational, considered to be the most outstanding exhibit ever of taxidermy as an art form. The winner was Frank Newmyer. In 1984 the World Taxidermy Championships held a competition called the Master of Masters. The winner was Frank Newmyer.

It was at the 1984 competition that Frank took four Best-in-World titles. Over the years he has earned seven best-in-show awards. Unlike other competitions, only one such prize is given per contest. He has also won seven People's Choice titles and twenty out of twenty-eight best-of-category awards.

In 1984 Frank became the youngest taxidermist to be inducted into the Taxidermy Hall of Fame. In 1985 he was described as the finest taxidermist in the world by wildlife photographer Peter Johnson of South Africa, and he appeared in Johnson's book, *The World of Shooting.*

By 1985, Frank Newmyer had taken 63 first-place ribbons in various competitions and had received the *Taxidermy Review*'s Distinguished Taxidermy Award six times.

Because of his knowledge of ornithology, Newmyer has made a significant contribution to wildfowl carving and painting. More than a dozen major flatwork artists have executed state and federal duck stamps using his mounts as references. They include David Maass, Larry Hayden, Heiner Hertling, Harry Antis, Russell Cobane, Richard Timm, and Jim Foote. And easily as many carvers have won major competitions using Frank's mounts, including Pat Godin, Howard Nixon, Steve McKoy, Randy Tull, Clark Sullivan, Tim Borque, Jon Jones, and Bob Perrish.

When not doing taxidermy work, Frank may be writing for such outdoor publications as *Breakthrough* and *Wildfowl Carving and Collecting* magazines. Or he may be found in Alaska, studying eiders in their natural environment; or sculpting a larger-than-life

Newmyer working on the wood duck mount featured in this book.

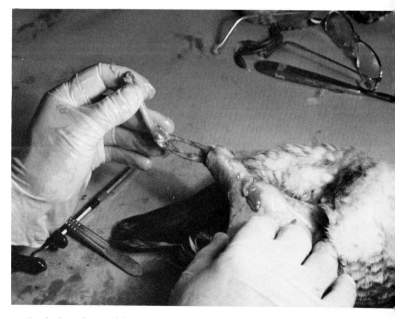

As Frank skins the wood duck, he helps the reader understand the anatomy. He is holding the humerus bone in his left hand. Attached to that are the ulna and radius. These bones are part of the wing skeleton.

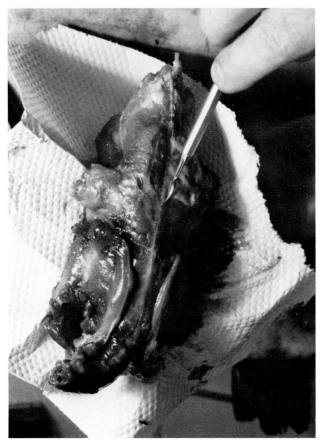

The skinned carcass of the duck (back view).

The wood duck project begins with skinning the waterfowl. Step-by-step photos like this one make the process clear and simple.

gamebird; or coming out with better products for the taxidermist or wildlife artist.

This book describes the personal story of Frank Newmyer, from his years as a youthful taxidermist to his observations of nature to his role as wildlife designer.

It then presents a project done especially for the book. The subject is a wood duck, a bird strikingly colorful and common throughout much of the United States. Tips on bringing it in from the field and freezing the bird are given, followed by a thorough explanation of and photographs on removing the skin. Readers are shown how to clean the skin meticulously and mount it using a mannikin system especially designed by Frank. This system is being used by more and more of the 20,000 or so taxidermists in the United States. Cost-effective and simple, it has been a major breakthrough for the taxidermist preserving gamebirds.

After describing the mounting, the book proceeds with details on painting the feet and bill. Because Frank has designed and produced artificial body parts to replicate these portions of the anatomy, they are no longer subject to deterioration.

Tips follow on dealing with eyes and eyelids, after which the book tells how to make a habitat for the duck. The habitat will be what Frank describes as a backwater scene, a place that wood ducks are especially fond of. The materials used are easily obtain-

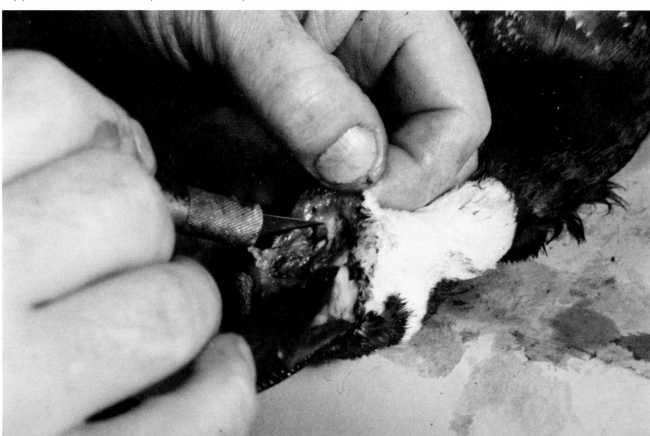

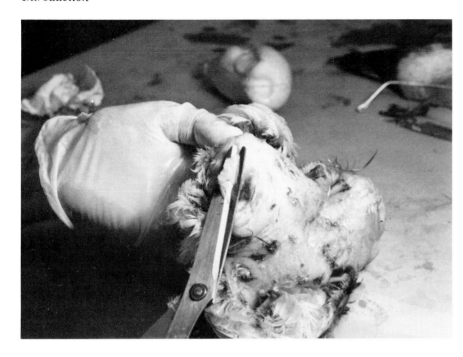

Once the skin, skull, and carcass are separated, the fat must be entirely removed from the skin. Frank uses scissors for the procedure.

Another step in the fat removal. Frank uses a degreasing agent from Wildlife Designer Series.

After the degreasing, the skin is tumbled in sawdust and blown dry.

There are two ways of making a body to replace the carcass. One is the traditional way, using excelsior or wood wool and string. The other is to use one of Frank's mannikins. All mannikins are cast in a rigid foam.

Frank has also introduced artificial feet that are used in place of real ones, which will deteriorate over the years. He has also printed the Mannikin Companion Photo Series *for the taxidermist and wildlife artist. Many unique products are featured in the book.*

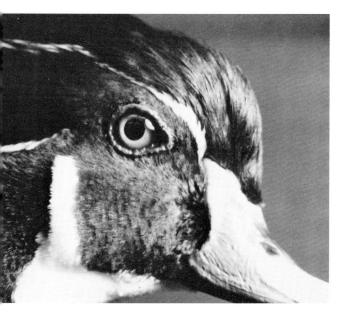

Glass eyes are used, but Frank adds to the realism by making the fleshy eye rings on the wood duck. (See chapter 7.)

able, and the step-by-step techniques are simple to follow.

Also included are a chapter on preserving feet and wings for later reference and a chapter on the aviary, a place to keep live birds for reference and later mounting. Tips on building the aviary and raising birds can be found in that chapter.

Next come comments from three wildfowl carvers who have used Frank's mounted birds to win an impressive number of competition titles and awards.

In the final chapter, "The Wildlife Designer Gallery," you will see many works by Frank, with explanations of their design and composition.

I have spent the last six years studying bird carving, working with such masters as John Scheeler, Grainger McKoy, Robert Guge, Ernest Muehlmatt, Jett Brunet, William Koelpin, Larry Hayden, Marcus Schultz, and Jim Sprankle. I have seen the bird in wood, and now I have seen the mounted bird. Clearly, Frank has provided new insights into what bird art can accomplish.

This is undoubtedly the first book to examine the excellence that taxidermy has achieved since the beginning of this decade. I hope it will lead to others, for taxidermy has just found new avenues of exploration—and Frank Newmyer has been one of the first to travel them.

Roger Schroeder
Amityville, New York

The mount is placed in what Frank describes as an Executive Case. A mud bank and murky water will be added later. The limb gives height and adds interest to the composition.

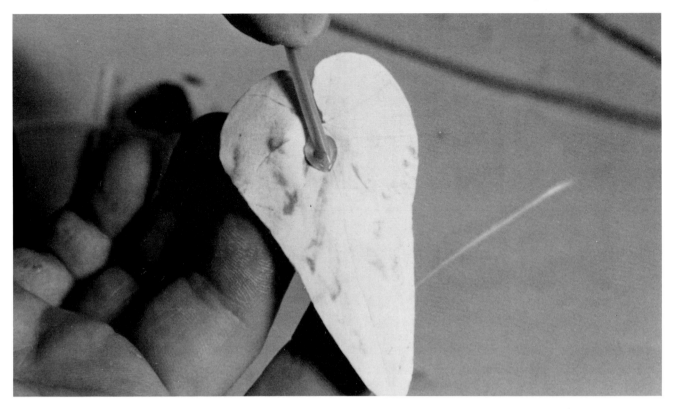

Part of the habitat will be aquatic plants. He shows the reader how to make arrowhead plants using plastic tubing, wire, and paper.

Frank shows how to place the plants in the composition.

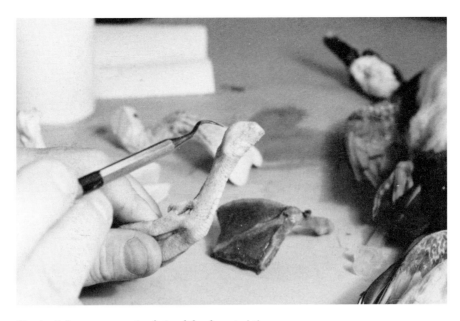

Chapter 9 discusses preserving feet and the characteristics of waterfowl feet. Frank is holding a cast foot.

Saving wings can be useful to the wildlife artist. This is a wood duck wing mounted so that the flight feathers and coverts can be studied.

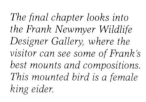

Chapter 10 deals with building an aviary and maintaining the wildfowl in it.

The final chapter looks into the Frank Newmyer Wildlife Designer Gallery, where the visitor can see some of Frank's best mounts and compositions. This mounted bird is a female king eider.

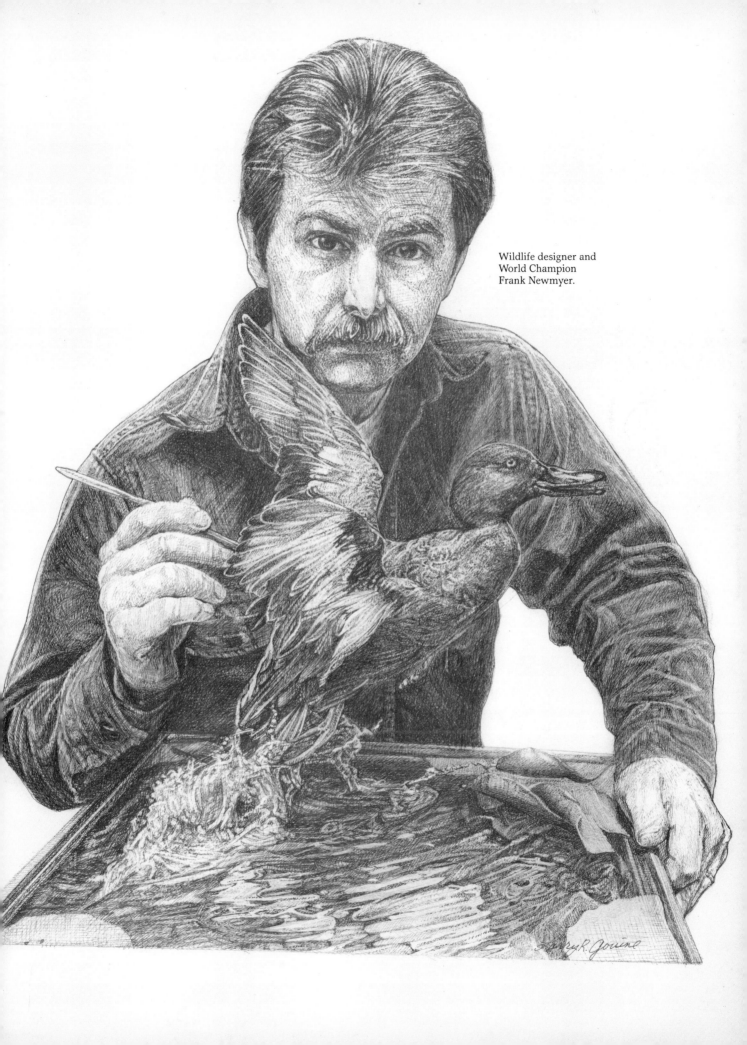

Wildlife designer and
World Champion
Frank Newmyer.

1

Frank Newmyer, World Champion Wildlife Designer

Since the age of seven, Frank Newmyer has been hooked on animals and on taxidermy. His introduction to the craft came through his father. A sportsman who enjoyed mounting the animals he had hunted, Joseph M. Newmyer ran a tool and die shop, but taxidermy was his hobby. Frank took up his father's interest eagerly. He mounted everything he could, and he earned a diploma from the Northwest School of Taxidermy at the age of twelve.

It wasn't long before Joseph Newmyer was operating a taxidermy business out of his home. He and Frank established a minimuseum there with mounted birds, painted backgrounds, and artificial marshes. Frank says of those early years, "It was creative for me to go outside and see something in the wild and then bring it in and recreate it." But the basement, where those re-creations were being made, was too small, so Frank's father found a separate shop for commercial work. It was called the Michigan Wildlife Studios, in Union Lake, Michigan. By the time Frank was in high school, he was running it in his spare time.

Running the shop was, in fact, part of his high school curriculum, and Frank was in it every day, learning the commercial aspects of taxidermy. But taxidermy work was seasonal for the Newmyers. During high school Frank also played drums in a rock band, and his group even made some records. But being a musician was not what Frank wanted to do in life.

His first real business was airbrushing scenes on vans and motorcycles. He believes this experience set the stage for his later work as an artist. In 1970, while he was painting, Frank married his wife, Linda, and they had two children, Frank Jr. and Jaemi.

In 1978 Frank decided to work full time as a taxidermist, specializing in birds. He chose wildfowl for the beauty of birds, their colors and forms. With birds, he felt, he could do his most creative work.

Owing to early experimentation with dioramas, Frank saw the artistic potential of gamebird taxidermy. What he has been doing, he says, is taxidermy that incorporates natural history. But, he adds, he

Typical of Frank's remarkable compositions is this trio of wood ducks in a corner case.

A green-winged teal in an Executive Case. The habitat of plants and earth was made from such materials as resin, paper, and plastic.

*A female wood duck.
The water was made from
Plexiglas with
a coating of resin.*

A remarque by Frank Newmyer, World Champion.

seeks good design and "an artistic flair."

Frank, who now lives in Gladwin, Michigan, a wooded and lake-filled area 150 miles northwest of Detroit, believes that professional taxidermy can be divided into three areas: commercial, custom, and museum taxidermy. The commercial variety, he says, is for hunters who want to preserve a specimen without a large investment. Custom taxidermy is for the people who are looking for a piece that brings together natural history and art.

Frank calls himself the World Champion Wildlife Designer, and in his workshop some of the finest examples of bird mounts and dioramas with manmade

habitat have been created. All exhibit a meticulous fidelity to detail. In a separate building that is both showroom and museum are many mounts that Frank has kept for himself. One remarkable composition depicts a great horned owl in a life-and-death battle with three crows. The setting is winter, and the owl fights off its attackers on a pine branch with dead limbs and frost-covered needles. One crow is already dead, another is in the talons of the owl, and the third crow clings to the back of the bird of prey. The outcome is hardly in doubt: Frank says that the great horned owl is the master of the skies.

Frank first did the piece when he was a teenager, then mounted new crows and chose a different setting. In 1984, it won the title that gave it its name: "Master of Masters."

Another piece, entitled "Only for a Moment," depicts three oldsquaws flying over Alaska's Ching Poot Bay. A remarkably convincing landscape of birds and artificial habitat, it won the Carl Akeley Award at the 1983 World Taxidermy Show held in Atlanta.

One large piece in Frank's showroom conveys the chill of a part of the Pacific coast with a sheet of ice hanging from a vertical cluster of rocks. There are six ducks in the scene, four Barrow's goldeneyes and two common goldeneyes, along with simulated barnacles and mussels and even water in which two of the Barrow's goldeneyes swim. The piece is titled simply "On the Rocks."

Still another impressive piece incorporates a rare white ruddy duck running across water as it is chased by a drake ruddy. The bird's feet splash over the resin-and-plexiglas surface, and some resinous water is on the white breast. As Frank points out, "You see not just the ducks. You see all the elements of the pursuit and the mood that it creates."

These masterpieces of drama, animation, and setting are typical of what Frank can do. But what is the secret to achieving such lifelike compositions? Research is part of the answer. "You have to study live birds continuously," Frank advises. He not only goes to parks, zoos, and wildernesses, such as Alaska, but he also has an aviary with over thirty waterfowl in it, as well as pheasants and quail.

"I concentrate on the basics," he explains. "These include the feather groups and the bird's muscles, skeleton, and bone details." The study method, he says, is not unlike that of the great masters of painting, such as Leonardo da Vinci and Michelangelo. They studied anatomy from the inside out. "You can remove static impression and create movement only by knowing the bird."

According to Frank, some taxidermists concentrate on quantity, producing a great deal of work with no character in their mounts. But Frank looks to create not only character but also animation. "Other taxidermists will just stuff a bird and put it on a limb, whether it belongs there or not. When they do that, it shows that they don't know or care about a bird's habitat or behavior. The results are boring."

How might Frank arrive at a composition with a dynamic design? Canvasback and wigeon ducks will be in dispute when feeding in the same area, he has observed. The dispute may be over a piece of eelgrass. The canvasback is a diver and will retrieve the grass from deep in the water; the wigeon can't dive as deeply, and it wants the grass. A struggle over the food ensues, each duck pulling an end of the grass with its bill. Which duck will keep the grass is unclear as the water around them is riled up. It is a typical waterfowl composition, which Frank has created using two mounted birds and water made of catalyzed resin and acrylic plastic. He has entitled it "The Robber," and it depicts Frank's deep understanding of behavior.

Frank buys many of his birds from licensed game breeders, and others are brought to him by sportsmen wanting their specimens mounted. Some Frank has hunted himself. When hunting, he says, he maintains a conservationist ethic. Much of what he shoots will be preserved, and his hunting is not wasteful.

Frank and "Marsh Maestro,"
a gift to Ducks Unlimited of Canada.

The work that is not done for hunters usually goes to such galleries as Wild Wings Decoy Den, Orvis Gallery, and Collectors Gallery. Gallery owners who have been particularly helpful to Frank are Andy Andrews and Kal Jabara.

He feels that he has been blessed by God in his artistic abilities. His work is an acknowledgment of and a thanks for these talents. His mission, he says, is to recreate nature with beauty and dignity, as God intended it to be observed by man.

There are between 8,500 and 9,000 species of birds in the world, and Frank says he would feel honored if he could mount even a thousand of them. Yet he believes that there are other ways of preserving birds. Bronzes are one way; birds carved from rigid foam are another. He recently constructed a flying mallard duck, three times the size of the real bird, for Ducks Unlimited of Canada. It is a copy of their logo, and it is made from the same rigid foam used to make portions of his habitat displays.

Frank sees himself as an artist who can handle many mediums. In fact, he believes that the only difference between his work and that of a sculptor is that he uses skin instead of wood or bronze. His taxidermy utilizes all the elements of other art media, from sculpting to painting to carving to detailing habitats.

"Bronzes and carvings are more appreciated by the uneducated," Frank says. "Yet there are those who will say that a bronze is fine art but a carving isn't. What is the difference? If I take a carving and make a bronze from it, am I then a fine artist?"

Frank has taught seminars in which he has asked students whether they consider taxidermy an art form. The majority of hands go up. He then asks the students whether they sell their work as art. Few if any hands are raised. Frank points out that very few taxidermists have had any training in art, which to him means design and composition.

Ironically, Frank plans a future composition that has no birds but a shark in it. Frank has been interested in predation for as long as he has been doing taxidermy. That is why he wants to collaborate with wildlife artist Tom Wolf to recreate the confrontation of two predators: a great white shark and a man, a skin diver in a wet suit. The composition would enact the moment before the shark consumes the human, when the force of the shark is hitting him. No blood would be depicted; perhaps the diver's mask would be torn off. Frank plans to display this life-size drama in a case

with portholes for viewing.

For the last several years, however, much of what Frank has been creating has featured serene compositions, such as the wood duck mounted for this book. It is in a relaxed pose in what Frank describes as "a utopian setting for a duck." He adds, "It gives people the opportunity to think about being a non-predatory animal like a duck when they themselves are predators on land, in the air, and in the water."

Whatever the composition, Frank's primary job is to capture a bird in its lifelike state. He begins by removing the skin as if he were a surgeon. After careful preparation, he will either make a body out of excelsior or wood wool, or he will use a rigid foam mannikin, one he has introduced to the field. After taxiing the skin, he will lock it in place while it dries. Adjustments are made so that the bird looks not only true to its species but also lifelike.

Then habitat comes into play, and this is where Frank the wildlife designer truly emerges. The composition may be a piece of the woods, a stream, the ocean, a tree, or a backwater scene, one typical of the wood duck shown later in the book. The bird must be part of its natural environment, and Frank is one of the best in doing what might be described as taxidermy landscapes.

So a wood duck preens on a muddy bank near water. Or a ruddy duck skims across the water. A group of oldsquaws will wing their way across an icy marsh. Frank is doing portraits of wildfowl.

Though Frank has composed such large pieces as "Master of Masters" and "On the Rocks," he primarily does what he calls the Executive Case. This is a base with a glass case that measures 12 by 22½ by 14 inches high, typically displaying a single standing or sitting gamebird in a microcosm of habitat: moss, grass, leaves, a wood snag, perhaps brackish water. Frank says the Executive Case is his best seller.

Despite the natural appearance of these displays, nothing in their composition is left to chance. Everything is arranged to give a pleasing design. A branch is chosen not only for its color but also for the artistic lines it contributes to the overall composition. Leaves are chosen not to fill up space but for color combination and complement. There is no clutter: everything is there for a purpose.

Praise for this kind of work has come from many quarters. In a letter from Peter Johnson, the South African author of *The World of Shooting*, Johnson writes: "There is no doubt, and there never was, that you are in a league of your own as an artist and I just wish that you lived a little closer to us here in Africa. Your work is so good that were I God, I feel that by simply puffing my breath at any one of your pieces, they would take wing and fly away!"

Frank sent Robert Bateman, one of the finest wildlife artists alive today, a gift of a mounted hooded merganser. In appreciation, Bateman wrote, "It is absolutely superb and an object of constant admiration."

It is no wonder that so many artists and carvers have sought out Frank to mount birds they wanted to paint or recreate in wood. Two of them have been Larry Hayden and Jim Foote, well-known Michigan carvers who turned their skills to painting wildlife. Frank met these artists when he began to display his work in Michigan sportsman shows in 1977. Early on Frank was preparing birds in their natural attitudes of sleeping, waddling, preening, and looking serene. His pieces stood out above the rest, and he captured the attention of these two artists.

Hayden had taken an unprecedented number of consecutive best-in-show ribbons with his carved waterfowl in early competitions. But he soon turned to painting birds, and he designed duck stamps for Michigan, Nevada, and Texas. He approached Frank for mounts and shared with him his knowledge of birds.

Foote, who was a wildlife biologist for twenty-seven years before retiring to focus on carving and painting, was also impressed with Frank's taxidermy. He, too, shared with Frank his knowledge of waterfowl anatomy and behavior.

Frank speaks highly of both men and of what they taught him. He says simply, "They schooled me on feather anatomy."

Frank was also close to John Scheeler, seven-time World Champion of carved wildfowl. Frank made mounts for Scheeler, and they communicated with each other until Scheeler's death in 1987. Frank says that John's work was original, that his gift was "in tune with the basic things in life." He adds, "Anyone who was good and original like John will be long recognized as a great artist."

Competitions were important to artists like Hayden, Foote, and Scheeler, for it gave their work exposure and recognition. The same was true for Frank. Winning championships helped give him credibility, he says. But he stopped competing with other taxidermists in 1986. Now he judges at most major competitions.

The seminar has replaced the contest for Frank. There he can instruct taxidermists in the art form. Although he travels to different states to teach, now he is giving four-day courses at his home in Michigan,

Among Frank's contributions to the field of taxidermy are the mannikin and artificial body parts.

Frank's mannikins and body parts, such as feet, necks, and heads, are cast in a rigid foam and are anatomically accurate. This is a mannikin for a ring-necked pheasant.

where taxidermists can learn mounting and habitat preparation and study birds in the aviaries Frank has on his property.

Whether at competitions or seminars, Frank is usually asked to evaluate the work. He starts by asking about the reference material. Many taxidermists use only pictures, and many more have never seen the live bird they are mounting or carving. He doesn't discourage the use of photographs, but he says photos aren't enough. "A picture of a bird is cold until you study its body language," he states categorically.

Years ago, Frank says, "I realized that not being around live birds made it extremely difficult to get an understanding of what my photo references were telling me. I was just looking at a flat surface. I couldn't tell what was happening on the other side of the bird, for example. So when I studied birds I took photos from all angles."

Still, there are limitations with the camera, particularly for the carver of wildfowl. The highly animated poses that many carvers look for are often split-second movements that are hard to capture on film, and lighting can distort anatomy and cast shadows suggesting features that just don't exist.

"The limitations of a camera become apparent to the top carvers, and that's where my knowledge can come in. I can explain the nuances of anatomy, and my mounts offer three-dimensional models that allow the carver to anticipate problem areas and avoid artistic license. They can see feather layout and patterns, and they have a painting reference."

Whether competing or creating pieces for the public, Frank has worked hard to develop his own style. He has done so not by comparing his work with what other taxidermists are doing but by relying on his memory of the real bird and the positions it took. That approach has also helped him get the "stiff" look out of a mount.

"You can't do the taxidermy I'm doing unless you understand each bird's anatomy—how it moves, how the feather groups respond, how the wings work, the feet move, the muscles contract—and the environment the bird lives in. Many taxidermists don't realize that to put the live feeling into taxidermy they have to approach it this way."

It is not surprising that Frank's energy in observing wildfowl should have led to innovations in the way birds are being composed. He believes he has come up with more innovations for the taxidermy industry than anyone else, numbering his contributions at fifty. Among them are accurate bird mannikins, artificial heads and bills, a system that locks the skin in place on a mannikin, artificial habitat, and recently videotapes on design and composition and what he calls the body language of the gamebird.

Frank sees taxidermy work as having a long life, unlike the popular conception of it. "Because of what taxidermy has been outside of museums, people think this work will last only a short time," Frank says. Prolonging the life of the piece is a major reason why Frank introduced artificial body parts. Unless there is breakage or the skin has long contact with direct sunlight, a taxidermied animal can last as long as a paint-

ing, a carving, or maybe even a bronze.

Frank has also used inorganic materials in making habitats more permanent. Plastics, metals, foam, sculpting compounds, and paper have replaced real leaves, vines, water, plants, and rocks.

There is no doubt that a love of the outdoors is key to Frank's career as an artist and innovator. "I never get bored going out into the woods," he says, and adds that kids today need too much hi-tech entertainment. "I'm a rare breed that can be entertained by His creations, not man's."

Frank says taxidermists, hunters, and wildlife artists can get better acquainted with themselves by learning about the outdoors. "Too many go out with a single goal in mind. For the hunter and a lot of taxidermists, it's to shoot the animal. For the artist it's to get a quick sketch or a photograph. And that's all they look for. But there are feelings that go beyond that. There are feelings to be gotten in the marshes and woods and bays that can make you bubble up inside until you feel like crying."

But he is troubled for the future of waterfowl. With the loss of wetlands to farming and housing, ducks have fewer and fewer places in which to breed: in this country alone, he says, we are losing 200,000 acres of wetlands a year. The duck is in trouble. And this is another reason why Frank continues to mount birds. They will be a reference for the future even as species become extinct.

But he sees some hope. Groups such as Ducks Unlimited have saved millions of acres of breeding grounds. And other groups have saved birds that were on the brink of extinction with special breeding programs.

What is Frank's contribution besides the mounts he makes? "Education is what it's all about," he says, and he will continue to speak out for the future of wildfowl. "God has given us this planet, and He has given mankind dominion over nature. This means He has given us the responsibility of preserving and respecting this planet."

2

Waterfowl Notes

There are 149 species of ducks, geese, and swans in the world. In North America alone over sixty species can be found.

No other group of birds has been so connected with civilization as have these waterfowl. People have hunted them, harvested their eggs, domesticated them, placed them in parks and aviaries. Waterfowl have inspired more literature than any other group of birds in the world.

At least four species of waterfowl have been domesticated, including the mallard in China two thousand years ago.

Most waterfowl are classified as migratory game-birds by the U.S. government and are subject to federal regulations. About 100 million ducks, geese, and swans migrate each year in North America, mostly southward from their northern breeding grounds. Many go as far as Mexico during the winter.

Migration has increased the flexibility of waterfowl. They can feed in northern climates, even tundras, and fly south to warmer climates in the winter. For ducks, this pattern means traveling great distances. The blue-winged teal, for example, nests in latitude 60 degrees north in North America and winters to beyond latitude 30 degrees south: a distance of over 6,000 miles.

The range in weight among ducks, geese, and swans is considerable. In this country, buffleheads and teal weigh about one pound, whereas a trumpeter swan can weigh as much as thirty pounds.

What keeps these birds related is their aquatic abilities. And the evolutionary adaptation for those abilities is the specialized leg, which ends with three front toes, connected with a webbing of skin, and a rear toe.

The rear toe is fleshier on diving ducks, such as canvasbacks, scaups, and oldsquaws, than on the so-called puddle ducks, such as mallards, gadwalls, pintails, and wood ducks. That rear toe helps in understanding the three types of feeding behavior that ducks have evolved. There are divers, like canvasbacks; surface feeders, called dabblers or puddle ducks (a wood duck is such a bird); and grazers, such as geese.

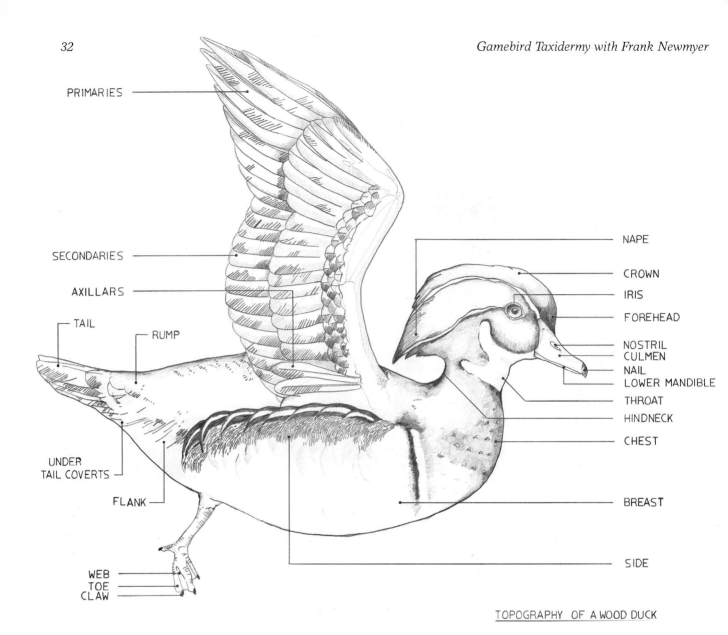

PRIMARIES

SECONDARIES

AXILLARS

TAIL

RUMP

UNDER
TAIL COVERTS

FLANK

WEB
TOE
CLAW

NAPE

CROWN

IRIS

FOREHEAD

NOSTRIL
CULMEN
NAIL
LOWER MANDIBLE

THROAT

HINDNECK

CHEST

BREAST

SIDE

TOPOGRAPHY OF A WOOD DUCK

The six species of divers in North America generally inhabit inland waters and feed primarily on seeds, leaves, and roots, while sea ducks eat invertebrates and fish. These sea ducks have large and powerful bills adapted for crushing mollusks and crabs. Except for them, divers are primarily freshwater species, though some winter on coastal waters. They characteristically have short wings and generally plump bodies. Many will go to considerable depths for food, and the oldsquaw will dive nearly 200 feet to feed. But compared with dabblers, they have shorter, pointier wings. Divers prefer water to land, and they need to "skitter," or run over the surface of the water, to take off. They require, then, a large area to become airborne, so they prefer larger bodies of water than dabblers.

Found throughout the world, dabblers make up the largest group of waterfowl, with fourteen species of dabblers in North America. These ducks feed on the surface or just below or on plant material on the bottoms of shallow ponds. This last behavior is called up-ending. Most are small with short legs and small feet. The hind toes of the dabblers do not have the flap or lobe common to divers. Yet the smaller dabblers can maneuver deftly in the air, and some can take off almost vertically from water.

The redhead drake, a typical diving duck. Some observers think that a diver's legs are farther back than a puddler's legs. This is not true. Compare the illustration with the next one. What creates the deception are the tail feathers, which are shorter on most divers.

The body of a gadwall, a puddler duck. Note how the legs come off the body at about the same location as on a diving duck.

A hooded merganser, another diving duck. Divers stand just as horizontally as puddle ducks, Frank explains. Compare with the next illustration.

A pintail, another puddle duck. Note where the legs come off the body, and compare with the previous illustration.

Grazing waterfowl like geese prefer grasses and pasture plants, though they will also feed in shallow water.

Whether they are dabblers, divers, or grazers, all waterfowl have what are called palmated feet. A duck, for example, is able to fold its toes and webs together to bring the foot forward through the water with little resistance. On the reverse stroke, the toes and webs spread apart to minimize drag.

Unlike our legs, birds' legs have three main sections. The femur, or thigh, is short and buried in muscle. It is joined to the tibia, which is comparable to our lower leg. Long and fleshy, it is known as the drumstick. The third and lowest section is the tarsus. Covered with scaly skin, it is the straight part of the foot above the toes. It can be compared to the arch of the human foot. It can bend not only forward but also backward.

Since there are no muscles to speak of on the leg, the parts must be controlled with a tendon system that acts like a pulley. One tendon runs around the back of the ankle joint and into the toes.

Another feature of a duck's feet is that they are rather far apart. The resulting waddle could be compared to a human trying to walk with a pillow between his legs. When a duck walks, the tail and the head move in the same direction, with the body weight shifting over the foot that is hitting the ground. The outer toe lifts up before the inner front toe when the duck takes a step.

Bird legs have an unusual adaptation that keeps them relatively unaffected by extremes in heat and cold. The arteries and veins are adjacent to each other, so the returning blood in the veins is warmed by the blood in the arteries, replacing lost heat. But very extreme cold will make the duck uncomfortable. This is why a duck will tuck its feet into the belly feathers when it is standing on ice or snow. Birds do not like to stand on snow anyway because ice buildup on their feet makes walking difficult. Yet a duck can stand on a hot stove for a long period of time and show little if any discomfort.

It has also been observed that a duck swimming in very cold water may have one foot tucked up in its feathers while the other is down, pushing the bird in a circle. The rotation helps prevent the water from freezing.

Looking at the toes of a duck, it can be seen that the inner toe is the fattest and fleshiest one—the duck pushes itself on this toe as it walks—and the hind toe is elevated.

A blue-winged teal hen. Note how the center toe angles inward.

On this blue-winged teal's feet, not all the toes and webbing are clutching what the feet are standing on. Most of the balance is achieved at the rear of the foot.

On this blue-winged teal drake, the rear of one foot is slightly raised while the rear of the other foot is down. This stance may help achieve balance.

The simplest way to tell whether a bird is a waterfowl or of another family of birds is to examine the bill. A waterfowl bill terminates in a nail. Yet bills can be very different in shape. A merganser, for example, has a long and thin bill with serrations, or toothy projections, that help hold fish. A shoveler has a wide bill for sifting water. And swans and geese have shorter, stiffer bills that aid with feeding on plants under water.

The bill of a duck is made up of two mandibles, or jaws. There is a soft, wrinkled covering, particularly on the upper mandible. The upper mandible is pierced by the nostrils, which are usually near the base of the bill. Inside the nostrils are nasal posts that help with respiration.

A duck's bill is wider than it is high. In scientific terms this formation is referred to as "depressed."

The bill has a variety of functions. It is a tool for touching, feeding, scratching, nest making, caressing a mate, and cleaning the feathers. It is, then, hand and mouth for a waterfowl. As a hand, it can hold and carry food or nesting material, and as a mouth, it can tear, crush, or cut food.

Colors are varied for ducks' bills. Mergansers' bills are orange-red; wood ducks' are multicolored.

Aside from feet and bills, what truly distinguishes

waterfowl and other birds from all other animals is the feathers.

Feathers do five things for a bird. They act as an insulator to keep in body heat. They create an airfoil and steering structure for flight. Feathers keep the bird waterproofed and protect the skin from injury. And their colors act either as camouflage or as signals for breeding.

It is very important that birds have feather insulation to control body temperature. Heat is retained by air that is trapped close to the skin by the feathers. When the outside temperature drops, the outer feathers are fluffed up to increase the warmth.

There are basically three types of feathers. Among the most important on a waterfowl are the contour feathers. These are the ones that form the outline of the body. They contribute to the streamlining of the bird in flight. It has been found that a bird can even change the shape of its body surface to increase streamlining.

Contour feathers grow in tracts. These tracts have a central quill, or rachis, from which projections called barbs spread out on either side. The barbs in turn have barbules, which interlock and keep the barbs together. When barbules come apart, a duck repairs the feather by rehooking the barbules, using its bill to "zip" up each row much as a zipper is locked together.

Flight feathers are long and wide, and they also have quills and barbs. These are on the wings and tail and provide the surfaces that enable a duck to fly. They are strong yet light. There are seven groups of feathers on a wing: the primaries, secondaries, tertials, middle coverts, lesser coverts, primary coverts, and axillars.

A bird can assume various feather "attitudes," depending on how nervous, active, or relaxed it is. When a bird is in flight, it is tight feathered. When a bird is nervous, its feathers are compressed tightly and are streamlined to its body, ready for a quick departure if necessary. But when the bird is relaxed, the feathers will lay loose and fluffy.

Down feathers have barbs but no barbules to lock the barbs together, which is why down is fluffy. Down feathers help keep the bird warm.

Though the number of feathers can be small – less than a thousand – for a bird like a hummingbird, a wood duck has about two thousand feathers, and a whistling swan has over 25,000.

Duck's feathers need to be cleaned, and a great deal of time can be spent doing this. A duck or any bird preens one feather at a time, working from the base to the tip, to repair split feathers and remove oil, dirt, and parasites. When preening, a duck rubs its bill in its preen gland, located at the base of the tail. Then it rubs preen oil over the surface of the feathers, giving special care to the flight feathers. Preening basically

When a duck stands on one leg, that leg is angled in for counterbalance. Note that the center toe lines up with the center of the breast.

Waterfowl waddle because their legs are short and placed rather far apart on their bodies. When a duck walks, it must be able to shift most of its weight over the foot that is hitting the ground. If it doesn't, the duck will lose its balance. The head usually swings in the same direction as the tail to achieve counterbalance.

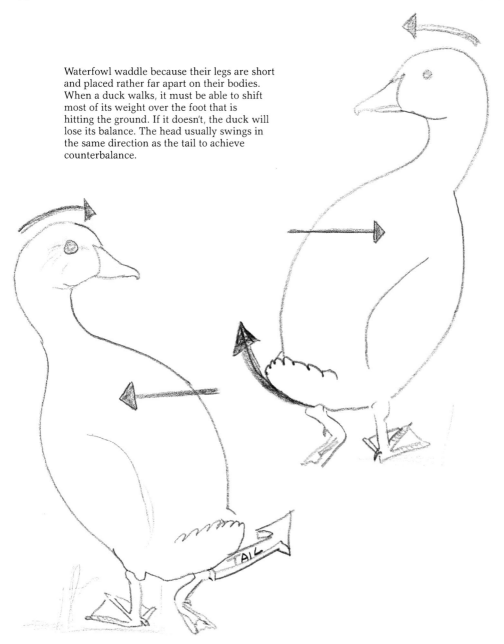

serves to waterproof the feathers and for ducks usually follows bathing. Ducks also use their feet for cleaning feathers, especially those on the duck's head.

Feathers have structural colors built into them, or they can have pigments. Structural colors are iridescent or noniridescent. Iridescent colors change according to how the light hits them, and they have a metallic look. They are formed either from a substance called keratin, a proteinlike chemical, or a material called melanin. Pigmented colors are found not only on the feathers but also on the bill, legs, and feet of a duck.

Colors on a duck have two main functions. They can camouflage or conceal the bird, or they can help others of the species to recognize it. Feather displays signal courting intentions, for instance, and plumage patterns can keep a flock together by special wing or tail patches that allow birds to follow each other while in flight.

The main purpose of camouflage is to make the bird

inconspicuous to predators. Since the female duck is the nest sitter, she is usually earth toned to blend in with the surrounding foliage. This coloration is sometimes called cryptic or protective.

The male may be brightly colored, as is the case with the wood duck, for mating purposes, but a male will undergo a period of what is called eclipsed plumage. Then the breeding plumage becomes drab looking until the new breeding season begins.

Ducks are also camouflaged by their light underbellies, which eliminate the darker color that would otherwise result from the bird's own shadow cast on its underside. Another trick of ducks is to crouch down to reduce conspicuously cast shadows.

Feathers get worn away because of abrasion with the ground or foliage. And since a full-grown feather can grow no further, it must be replaced. This replacing is called molting, and birds molt at least once a year. Molting is also a way of renewing worn or faded plumage. Ducks, unlike other families of birds, lose all their flight feathers at about the same time, so for a period they are flightless.

Despite this problem, flight has enabled ducks to reach almost every kind of habitat on the planet except Antarctica. Adaptation has enabled ducks to find not only new breeding grounds but also new sources of food. And, of course, new environments have shaped the forms and functions of duck anatomy.

Simply put, a bird evolved differently from a mam-

A redhead drake in a preening posture. The bill must be able to touch all parts of the body except the head in order to clean and repair feathers.

mal to enable it to fly. A bill replaced heavy teeth while the bones of the skull became thin, as did the leg and wing bones. Also, the wing and shoulder structure changed to accommodate the large flight muscles that run between the forearm and the keel, or breast.

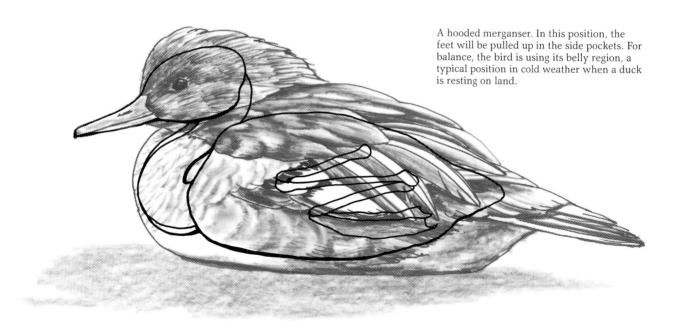

A hooded merganser. In this position, the feet will be pulled up in the side pockets. For balance, the bird is using its belly region, a typical position in cold weather when a duck is resting on land.

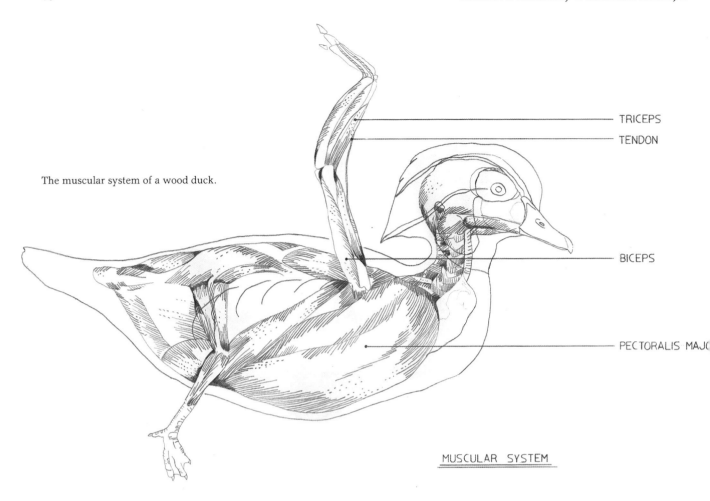

The muscular system of a wood duck.

TRICEPS

TENDON

BICEPS

PECTORALIS MAJ(

MUSCULAR SYSTEM

On the wings, the upper arm is called the humerus. The humerus fits into a cavity or socket and is comparable to a person's arm between the shoulder and elbow. Attached to it are the radius and ulna, which make up the forearm. The ulna holds the secondary flight feathers. Then there are the wrist and finger bones. These hold the primary feathers. Wings move with the pectoral girdle, and the wing sockets are braced by the clavicals, or collarbones, which point downward and form a tripod called the wishbone. The pectoral girdle is designed to withstand the stresses that are forced on the front of the body when the flight muscles contract.

The most important muscles are the two sets of flight muscles running between the humerus and the keel of the duck. One pair contracts when the wing is on the downstroke, and the other pair contracts when the wing is on the upstroke. These muscles can weigh as much as one sixth of the weight of the bird.

In order for a bird to fly, it must achieve what is called force lift, made possible by the bladelike shape of the wing. Air strikes the leading edge of the wing and divides. Because the upper surface of the inner part of the wing has the greater curvature, air travels at a greater distance than that on the underside. This differential in turn creates a lower pressure across the surface, and lift occurs.

Since wings cannot support the bird on the ground, the skeleton underwent changes to enable it to walk bipedally, or on two feet. Evolution shortened the backbone between the pectoral and pelvic girdles, bringing the bird's center of gravity to the rear of the body.

The skull for both mammals and birds is attached to the backbone, though on birds the bones of the backbone over the pelvis are fused to form the rigid body that is necessary for flight. On the other hand, the neck is more flexible and has more bones. The neck vertebrae in a duck number seventeen. In a human, the number is five.

A pintail drake. There are seventeen vertebrae in a duck's neck, which act like a string of beads.

The vertebrae in a duck's neck allow the neck to rest low on the body, giving the bird the appearance of having no neck at all. The upper portion of the neck will actually rest on the back of the body, and the bill may rest on the top of the neck. When a duck is in a relaxed, nonaggressive pose, the vertebrae will remain compact and close together, and the lower neck will tuck into the clavical area. The neck will resemble a gentle **S** curve.

The seventeen vertebrae act like a string of beads sliding back and forth as the duck uses its neck and head as counterweights in balancing, flying, and standing at rest. Also, they allow the bird to reach back over the shoulder to contact the preening gland.

Another view of a pintail and its "neck language."

A sleeping pintail that is lying down. Note the neck attitude.

Another position for a sleeping pintail. This bird is standing.

A standing redhead asleep.

In flight the neck reaches directly out from the body and undulates in a generally extended **S**.

A duck's eyes are a large part of its head, often outweighing the brain. But when observing a living bird, the viewer can see only a small portion of the eye: The largest portion is hidden by the lids and the skull.

A duck's eyes are supported by sclerotic rings. These are a series of bony plates that vary in size and shape, depending on the species.

Man's vision is considered equal to a duck's, but a duck seems to have faster vision in that it picks out details more quickly than a human. It has, then, a greater sensitivity for movement. And most ducks have good color vision.

Waterfowl have both monocular and binocular vision, meaning they can see straight ahead or side to side. A fovea in the center of the retina of each eye enables the bird to see straight out from the side of the head. The duck thus sees entirely different objects with each eye. But the binocular, or straight-ahead, field of vision is small.

All birds have two eyelids, upper and lower, which are folds of skin. When closing their eyes, daytime birds draw up the lower lid more. There is little movement of the upper lids. But for birds that are active at night, like owls, the upper lid is more active. So on ducks, the upper lid will be fleshier.

Ducks have a nictitating membrane, or "third eyelid." This is a transparent skin that is drawn across the eyes from front to back to clean them. Some ornithologists believe that when ducks dive or fly, the nictitating membrane plays a major role in protecting the eyes, much as goggles do. It is also believed that these membranes have built-in lenses that correct the focus of the eyes.

When observing waterfowl from the front, a viewer will notice how the top of the eye is slanted out farther than the bottom. Simply, it follows the contour of the skull, and it enables a duck or other bird to see front on when feeding.

When a bird eats, digestion occurs in a storage sac called the crop. There food is macerated or ground up before it enters a two-chambered stomach. In the first chamber food is chemically broken down; in the second the gizzard grinds the food. Ducks swallow small stones that help with this grinding.

Ducks eat a variety of foods, depending on the species. Some ducks eat fish, others mollusks, and many more live on plants, seeds, fruits, nuts, and even insects.

How is waste removed from a duck's system? Ducks defecate and urinate through the same opening, called the anus or vent. This is why bird droppings consist of both dark feces and a whitish material, the urine. The vent is also the opening for the reproductive system.

Many ducks form a pair that keeps them together for a season or more. After copulation they build a nest. Nest building is dominated by the female, and she will use sticks, grasses, paper, string and, for saltwater ducks, seaweed.

The two main strategies of nest building are making the nest inconspicuous and making it inaccessible.

Despite the obvious need for hiding the nest, duck eggs are not so inconspicuous. Many are light colored and easily seen from a distance, apparently enabling other species to recognize the eggs.

The incubation for waterfowl ranges from eighteen to thirty-nine days. Soon after hatching, the young are ready to swim.

Given this general information on birds and waterfowl, we can look briefly at the wood duck, a common waterfowl that breeds from southern Canada through the southeastern United States and winters as far south as Cuba.

Many consider the male "woodie" to be the most beautiful native North American duck species. His exotic look stems from the swept-back crest, a unique facial pattern, and a brilliant iridescence. Some have written that the duck appears to be arrayed for a wedding. In fact, its Latin name, *sponsa,* means "the promised one."

The wood duck's specific habitat is wooded swamps, rivers, forests, wood lots, and the borders of lakes and ponds.

A medium-sized dabbling duck, its length ranges from seventeen to twenty inches. The head has a striking green iridescence with a pattern of white stripes. The bill is white, red, and black, and the eye is an orange-red. The neck and breast are burgundy colored with flecks of white, and the feet are yellow-orange. The female is much less colorful. But she does have a distinguishing white patch around her eye.

The wood duck is an early spring migrant and arrives on its northern breeding grounds soon after the spring thaw. Looking for natural tree hollows or cavities, the female wood duck leads the male to the tree of the previous year, and if the nest hole is occupied, a site is sought nearby.

Wood ducks will nest as high as sixty feet above the ground, and they will nest in manmade boxes. The female will lay as many as fifteen creamy-colored to dull-white eggs, which may take as long as a month to hatch. Two months after that the young ducks are ready to fly.

A wood duck's diet consists primarily of vegetation. It prefers duckweed, wild rice, and aquatic vegetation. But it will also eat beechnuts, hickory nuts, acorns, grapes, and even insects.

Commercial gunners took many wood ducks, and stuffed woodies were common in homes of the early 1900s. The feathers were also used for trout flies. But when the Migratory Bird Treaty of 1918 was enacted, these waterfowl were protected from overhunting.

In today's world, given good health and protection, a wood duck can live from four to ten years.

3

Skinning the Gamebird

One of the most important aspects of avian taxidermy is the study of the inner body. Unfortunately, most taxidermists see only the skin. The bird has to be taken as a whole. That means understanding how the head and neck work together, how the wings are used, how the feet move, how the tail operates, and how the body itself works. All of these parts come together to create the entire mount.

Some of the terms the taxidermist should familiarize himself with before skinning the bird are the following:

Clavical – the shoulder blade

Caudal section – tail section

Femur – thigh bone

Tibia – lower leg

Tarsus – the "ankle"

Humerus – upper bone of wing

Ulna and Radius – two bones that make up the forearm of the wing

Vent – the opening for waste disposal and reproduction

Mandibles – the jaws

Pygostyle – tailbone at end of the bird's backbone

Carcass – overall body without the skin

There are some tips for caring for your gamebird in the field and at home before removing the skin. When in the field, the taxidermist should wipe off as much blood as possible and place cotton in the bird's throat. Blood and body fluids can be removed from the feathers; doing so takes several operations but cuts down on the cleaning process outlined in the next chapter. When handling the bird, the taxidermist should hold it by the legs, not the neck. The legs do not have feathers, which can be pulled off by rough handling. And preserving the feathers is what taxidermy is all about. To carry it home, the bird should be placed in a paper bag. The paper will absorb moisture and fluids. A plastic bag is not advised because the bird will sweat moisture on its feathers, which will make later cleaning difficult. A paper bag will also prevent excessive wear on the feathers.

Once the bird is home, as much blood as possible

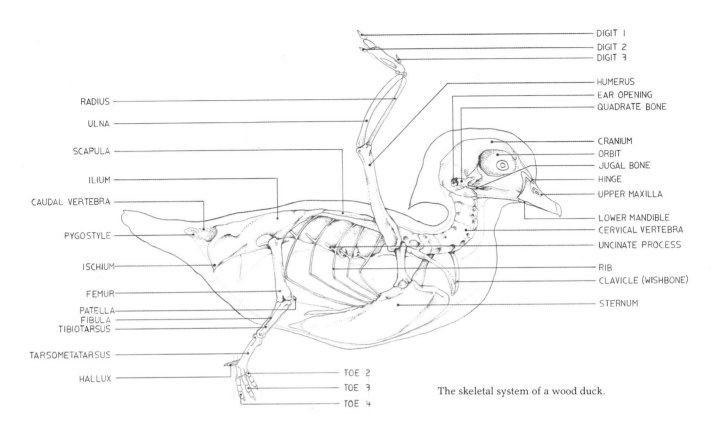

The skeletal system of a wood duck.

should be wiped off it. If the bird is not to be mounted right away, which is usually the case, then it has to be frozen. There are two ways of preparing the bird for the freezer. One is to place the head and neck over the back of the bird, and the other is to put the head and neck under one wing. The latter will definitely prevent the head and neck from being damaged or broken off if mishandled. A broken neck means torn skin and feathers. But whatever method is chosen, the bird should be placed in a plastic bag and sealed airtight. The plastic will hold moisture in. A zip-lock plastic bag is recommended.

Thawing is usually done overnight, but Frank says that a bird can be placed in a tub of hot water if the taxidermist is in a hurry. The bird can be skinned even when it is wet.

Some rules and regulations: Many states have laws limiting the length of time a bird may be possessed after the closing of the season for that species. Information required for each migratory bird in a taxidermist's possession includes the hunter's name, address, county in which the bird was taken, date shot, species and, if the bird was taken out of state, hunter's license number as well as his signature. The taxidermist

should keep a taxidermy ledger to record the data; most taxidermy supply companies carry them.

Taxidermy means removing the skin and arranging it on a new body. This approach, Frank wants to point out, is not the same as freeze-drying, a process that is being used by a number of taxidermists. The process involves taking a frozen bird, positioning it, propping it up on wires, and putting it into a vacuum that removes the water from it.

Freeze-drying, however, offers little longevity. In fact, in an environment with a great deal of humidity, the mount will go limp. The process is also a poor way to preserve the skin, since all the moisture is removed from it without other steps of preservation. And it does not discourage insects and bacteria from damaging the mount. The end result, Frank says, is an animal with the consistency of cardboard. So to do taxidermy, the taxidermist must be willing to remove the skin from an animal, sculpt the body or buy a mannikin, and taxi the skin on it.

For hygienic purposes, plastic gloves should be used. They should be tight fitting, for good touch is part of the skinning process.

For more hygiene-conscious taxidermists, the bird

Proper care of a bird to be mounted can begin in the field. A good preparation is to insert cotton in all the openings, including the vent, or anus, and the nostrils, to prevent blood clots and leakage. Blood and body fluids will not only stain the feathers, but they will also promote bacteria, which will cause the feathers to deteriorate later on. Here Frank places cotton in the throat of a wood duck. Openings should be stuffed before freezing a bird that is not to be mounted right away. Closing openings can also be done at home. Such preparation makes for a superior mount; the better the maintenance of the bird, the better the finished product.

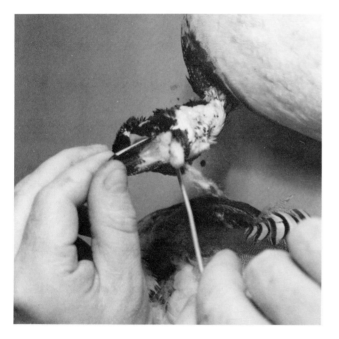

The wrong way to carry a bird in the field. Carrying the bird by its neck causes tearing of the feathers. The more you handle the feathers, the more damage you do. Also, never place a string around the bird's neck. It will actually pull feathers out.

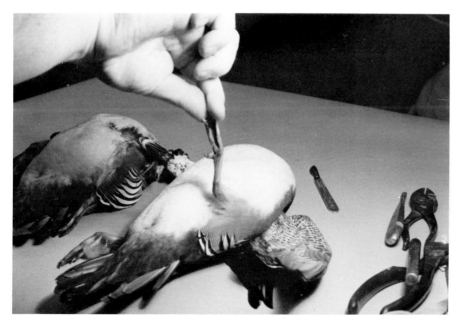

The right way to carry a bird in the field. Since there are no feathers on the feet, it makes sense to carry the bird by this part of its anatomy.

There are two ways to position a bird before freezing. One is to place the bird's head under a wing.

The other method of preparation is to place the head over the bird's back. Frank says either way is good, but he prefers the former method because the wing is a protector. If the head is hit sharply when frozen, it could break off. The same could happen to the bill. But Frank cautions that blood leakage must be stopped or blood will drip on the feathers under the wing.

Laws and regulations have been passed to help protect waterfowl from overhunting. In order for a commercial taxidermist to mount a client's legally shot waterfowl, the bird must have affixed to it a federal migratory bird tag. (See chapter 10, "The Aviary," for addresses of the offices of the U.S. Department of the Interior Fish and Wildlife Service.) The hunter must fill out this tag, and the taxidermist is required to keep it for at least five years.

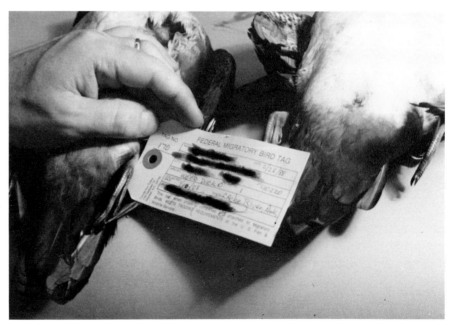

Two wood ducks ready for mounting. One is larger than the other. Size is dictated by maturity. Feather lengths will also vary. These birds were thawed slowly. Improper defrosting can cause damage to the tissues under the feathers and make skinning difficult.

can be skinned in a flat pan of cornmeal or preferably granulated borax, available from most taxidermy supply companies. The latter will be used later to help with the cleaning and mounting, but both that and cornmeal will absorb blood and body fluids.

The first step is to remove the feet. They can be saved for future reference, pumped up with chemicals, as explained in chapter 9, or replaced with artificial, plastic feet. Whatever decision the taxidermist makes, removing the feet now will make skinning easier. Using wire cutters, he cuts where the feathers of the tibia stop and the scaly tarsus begins.

The taxidermist starts skinning the bird by laying it on its back for a ventral incision. Using a scalpel, he cuts from the sternum, which is at the top of the clavicals, to the vent. A separation of feather tracts on the breast feathers, beginning at the top of the sternum, is a convenient "trail" to follow when making the incision.

Next, he separates the skin and fatty tissue from the carcass. Though a beginner may have trouble, a skilled taxidermist should be able to make the separation with his fingers. The trick is to push against the body with the thumb and use the other fingers to pull gently at the skin at the same time. The fatty tissues should separate from the body without ripping the skin.

When the femur is reached, it is skinned down to the tibia. The femur must be separated from the carcass to allow the skin to separate from the body. But the tibia is left in the skin to give a connection when the artificial leg or real foot is attached to the body.

The tibia must be cleaned, which means using the scalpel to remove the flesh. If this is not done, bacteria will start to grow immediately, and the skin will deteriorate quickly.

The taxidermist must also remove the knob at the end of the tibia. The wire cutters will do the trick here.

Frank points out that the ventral incision goes to the

Though a bird's feet can be saved for the taxidermic mount, artificial feet have given taxidermists a replacement with indefinite longevity. Cast feet, made from a rigid foam, can be shaped and painted to look like real feet, which can easily deteriorate over the years. (See chapter 9, "References for Feet and Wings," for tips on saving real feet.) Artificial feet were developed by Frank Newmyer and are available as part of Frank's Wildlife Designer Series. This photo shows a painted wood duck's cast foot on the left and the real duck's shrunken foot on the right.

This picture shows an artificial foot in a swimming position on the left and a real foot on the right.

Frank points to the place where the skin of the foot and the feathers come together. This, the start of the bird's heel and the end of the tarsus, is where the leg must be severed regardless of whether it is used or substituted with a cast foot.

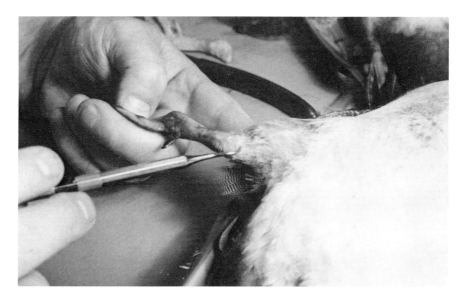

Heavy-duty wire cutters will remove the feet.

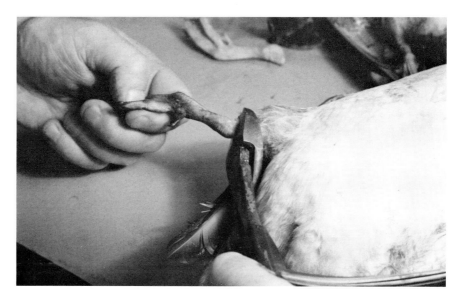

The foot removed. Note how much is left. The cut cannot be made across the feathers.

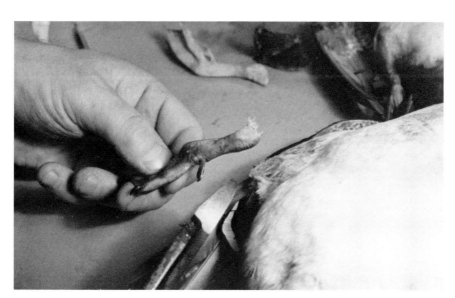

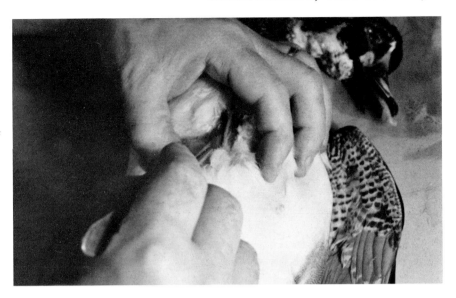

Using a sharp scalpel, Frank starts what is described as the ventral incision. This is the first major step in removing the skin. It is the incision most frequently used by taxidermists because birds have an area on their breasts that looks like a split. By cutting along this area, few if any feathers will be damaged. To find it, use your fingers to move the feathers apart. Note how Frank spreads the breast feathers with one hand while he starts the incision.

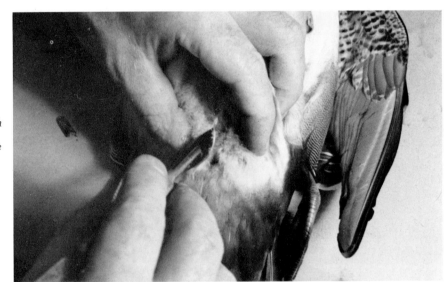

The scalpel must move down the sternum, which is the bone underneath the breast. It is not necessary to cut so deep that you grind the blade into the bone. Continue cutting until you reach the vent opening.

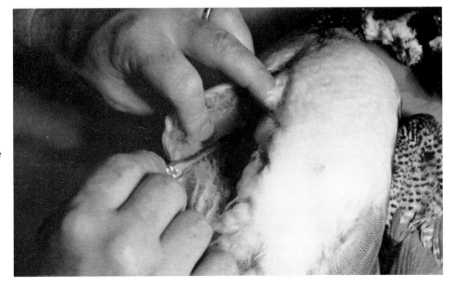

The next step in removing the skin is separating it from the body. Directly under the skin is a layer of fatty tissue that separates the skin from the carcass of muscles and bone. The skin and tissue can be pulled away from the carcass with the fingers, but Frank points out that doing so takes some practice.

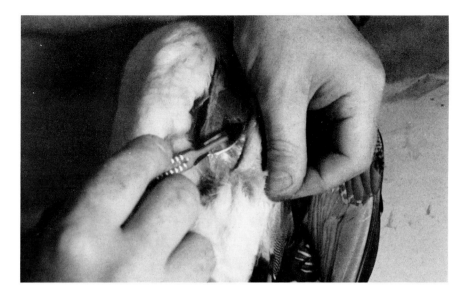

One hand can pull the skin and tissue away from the carcass while the scalpel scores the separation. But care must be taken that the skin is not ripped in any way.

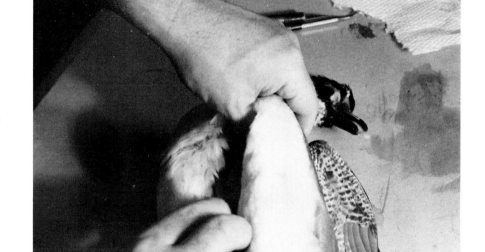

This method uses the thumb of one hand to gently pull the skin away from the body of the duck.

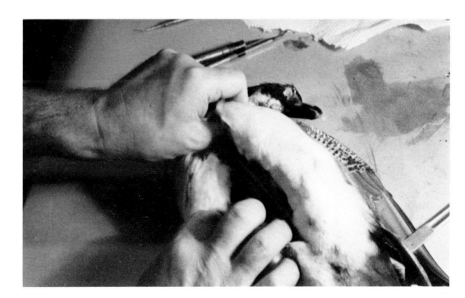

Again, the taxidermist must be careful not to rip the skin when separating it from the body.

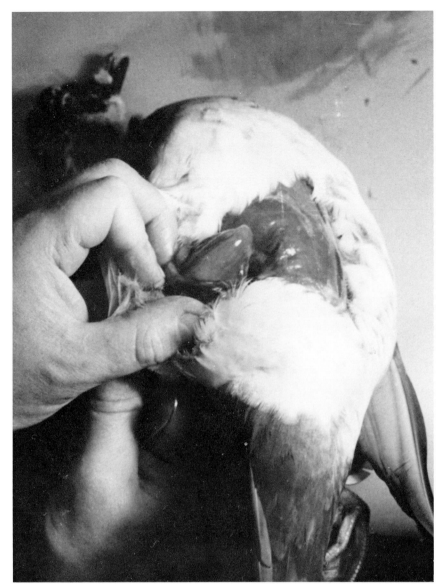

There are three parts to a bird's leg: the heel and foot, the tibia, and the femur. Since the foot was removed, the remaining joint is the tibia-femur connection. This must be exposed so that the two bones can be separated and the skin can be detached from the thigh meat.

If a cast foot is to be used, the femur becomes unnecessary and can be replaced with something more permanent, even a wooden dowel.

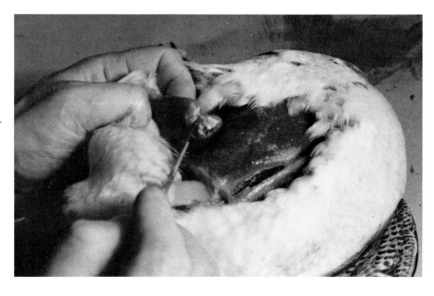

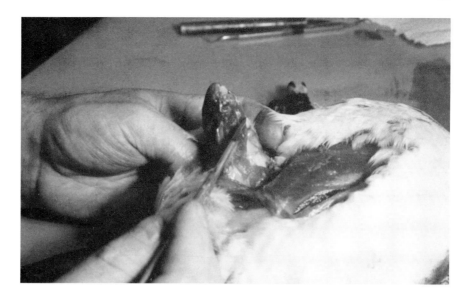

The bone that is left is the tibia. Since it will remain in the skin, it must be cleaned for hygienic purposes.

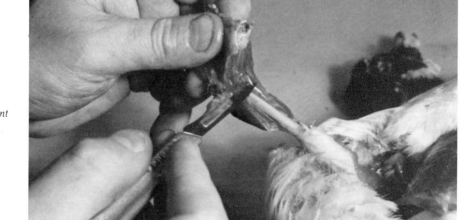

Removing flesh from the tibia. Meat left on it will cause bacteria to deteriorate the mount later on.

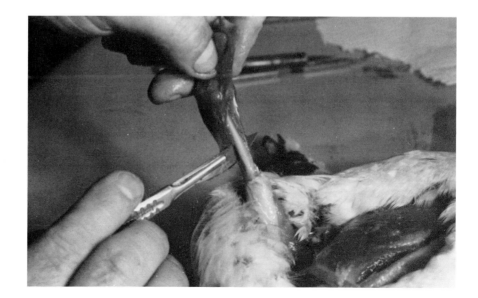

More flesh removal between the two bones of the tibia.

Now the knob of the tibia and the flesh on it can be removed. Heavy-duty wire cutters are used. Note how the bone is still connected to the skin.

Inside the bone there is marrow, which must be removed to prevent bacteria from forming. A heavy-gauge wire can be used.

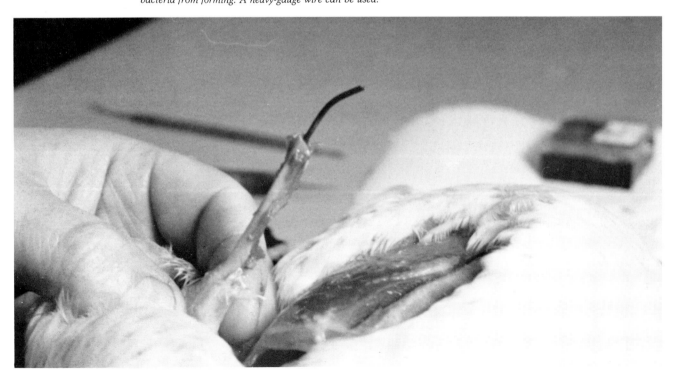

Exposing the tibia-femur joint on the other side. The scalpel blade indicates the joint that is to be severed.

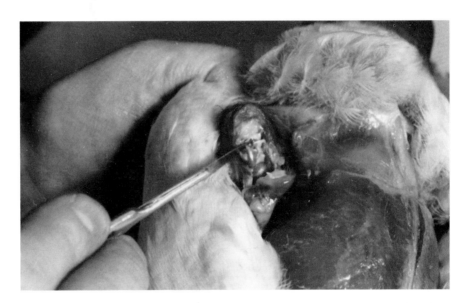

Cutting the joint with the scalpel.

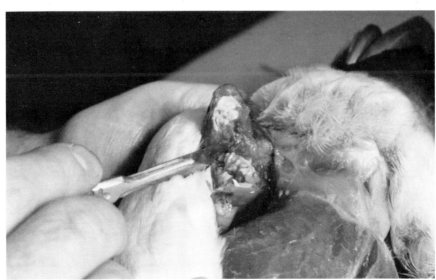

Continuing with the separation of tibia and femur.

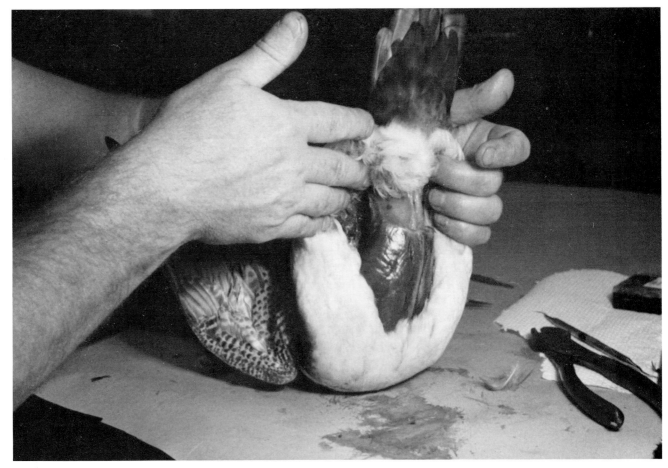

The next step is to lay the duck on its breast in preparation for separating the skin from the caudal section, or tailbone.

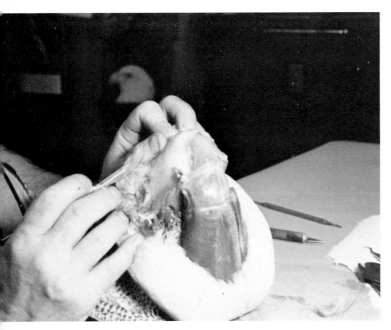

The skin must be pulled back up past the vent to expose the pygostyle, which is the very end of the fused vertebrae of the caudal section. This area is where the shafts of the tail feathers come together.

vent but not beyond it, since the skin beyond it can be removed with the hands. Less cutting means less stitching later on.

The bird then must be laid down on its breast so that the tail section can be dealt with. By holding the tail with one hand, the hand with the scalpel can start separating the tissue from the carcass. A joint that connects the pygostyle with the rest of the skin must also be separated with wire cutters.

Once the separations are made, the skin can be pulled over the pygostyle, and the skin can be separated from the back of the bird. The taxidermist has to be careful here because the skin is thinner on the back than on the breast, and it sticks more than in any other area.

After the tail section has been separated from the body, beginning taxidermists sometimes suspend the bird by tying a cord around the rear of the carcass and under the femur bones. They then pull the inverted skin down around the body toward the neck and head. Frank says that this method is more time-

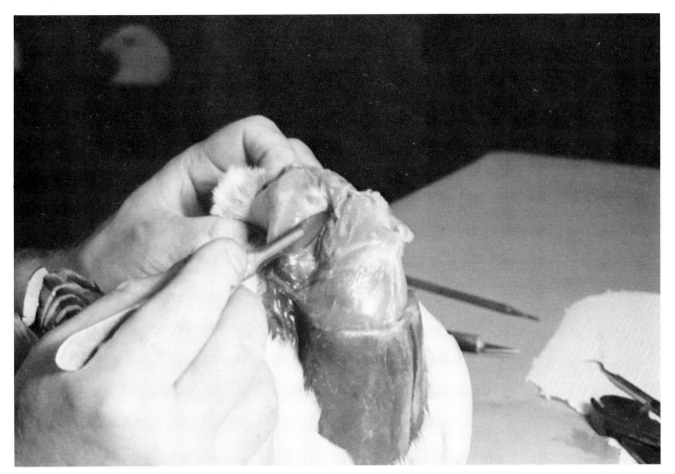

A scalpel must be used to start to separate the skin at this joint.

consuming than his, but the taxidermist can use it if he feels uncomfortable doing all the work with only his hands.

The next major step is to separate the wings from the body. The strategy is to separate them while preserving the flight bones. Were they removed, the wings would be too limp to mount properly.

The taxidermist first exposes the humerus joint, which is at the base of each wing, and severs it with the scalpel. He then continues with the skinning, going to the neck and head. The skin can be pulled down the neck to the base of the skull, and it should separate fairly easily without tearing.

Next, he frees the carcass from the skin where the neck meets the skull when the neck is cut away from the head. What is left is the skin with the head still in it. The necks on most waterfowl are too thin to allow the skin to be turned inside out over the skulls, which is why the cut is made. But on some birds, such as mergansers and eiders, reversing the skin can be accomplished.

The taxidermist should never make an incision through the side of the face or the top of the head to free the skin from the skull. This cut can leave an unsightly seam and ruin the look, especially on birds with crests or hoods.

Frank prefers to use artificial heads, ones that he has had cast and sells commercially. They are anatomically accurate, complete with bills. The only thing a taxidermist has to do, after inserting the skull, is paint the bill. For guidance, Frank has provided the *Mannikin Companion Photo Series,* an album of color prints.

Whether an artificial head or the real skull is used, the skin must still be separated from the skull, as it must be cleaned of all flesh.

The skin overlaps the bill on its sides and in V-shaped flaps on the top and back. Using the scalpel, the taxidermist can cut away these V flaps and release the skin. The same is done to the sides of the bill.

The skin should be separated as close to the bill as possible to keep the proper look to it later on. Part of the process of separating it is to peel it with one hand

Here Frank cuts into and separates the pygostyle from the skin.

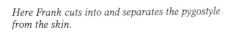

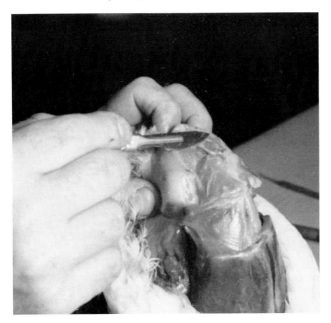

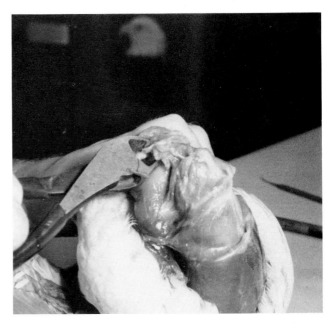

Pliers will be needed to finish cutting the pygostyle free, which will release the tail quills from the body.

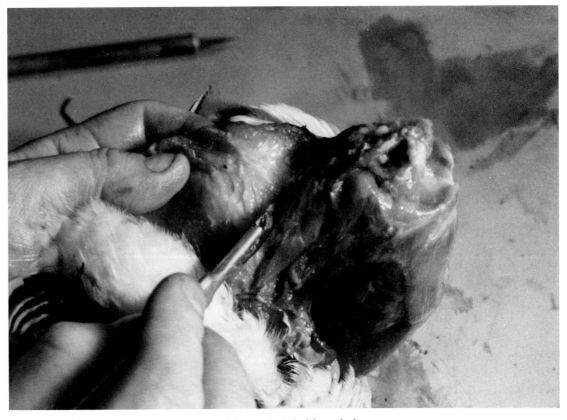

Here the remaining skin is removed from the pygostyle with the aid of the scalpel.

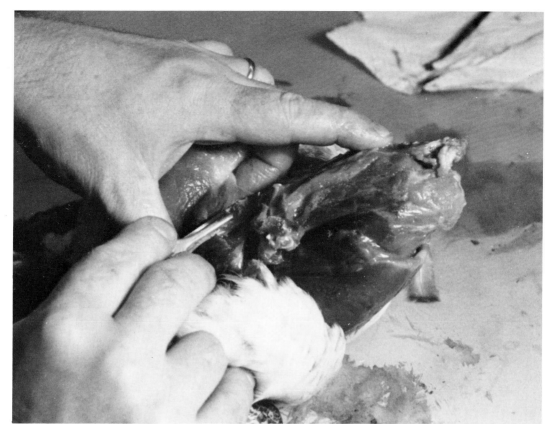

The skin must now be removed from the back of the bird. Caution must be exercised because the skin is thin on the back. It is advisable to use both fingers and scalpel.

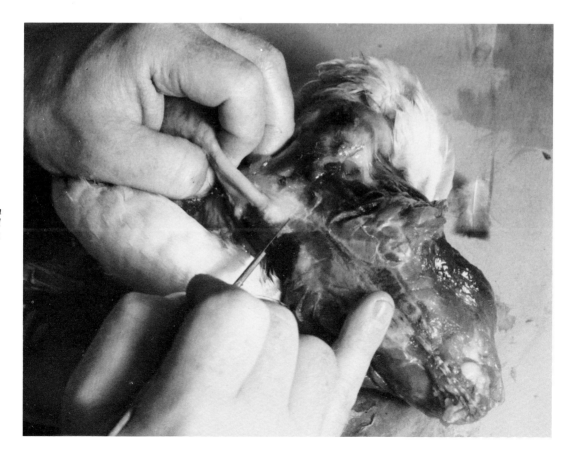

This photo shows skin tissue being separated from the carcass with the scalpel.

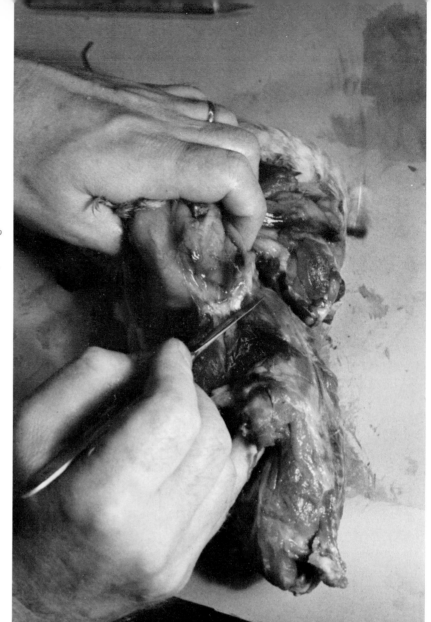

The next major step is to separate the wings from the body by exposing the humerus joint at the base of the body.

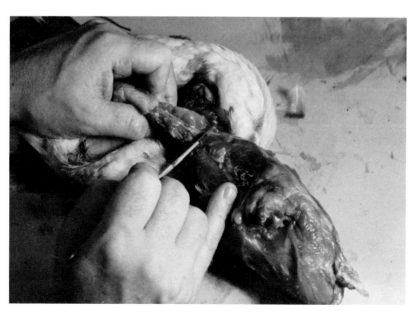

The humerus is severed with the scalpel. This procedure must be done for both wings. Be prepared to clean the wing bones of flesh for obvious hygienic purposes.

 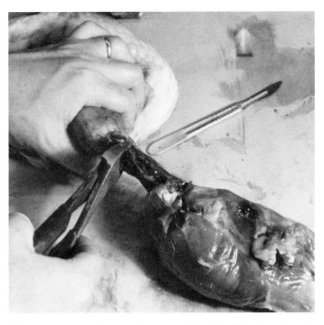

Next the skin must be pulled down the neck to the base of the skull. The skin should separate fairly easily, without tearing. Tears can, however, be sewn up once the skin is mounted on an armature or mannikin.

Wire cutters are used to sever the carcass from the skin where the neck meets the skull.

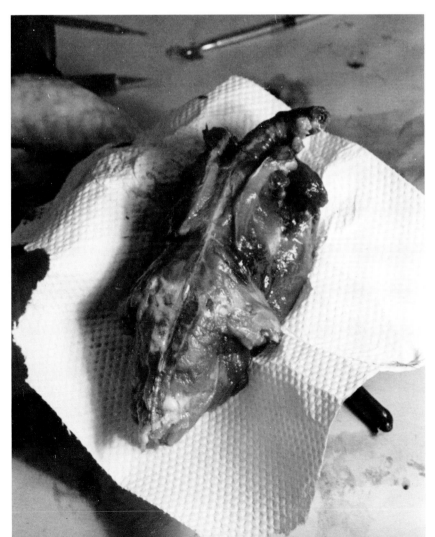

This is what the wood duck carcass looks like. The neck is at the top of the photo, the pygostyle at the bottom.

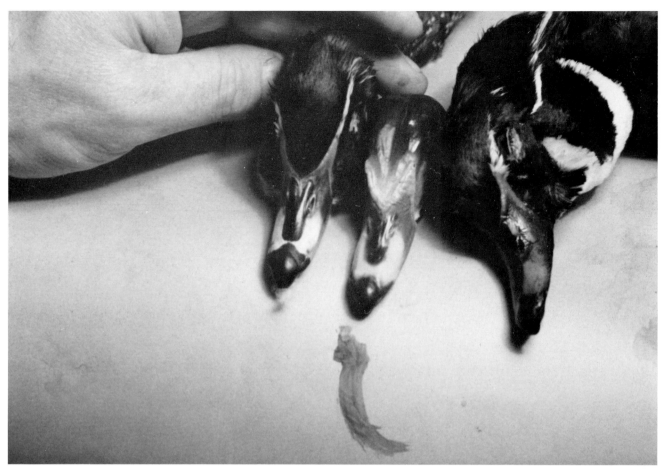

Before Frank introduced artificial heads, the inside of the skull of the bird had to be cleaned and used in the skin. If the skull were not cleaned, bacteria would spread and insects would ultimately get at the mount and destroy it. Here Frank compares one of his artificial heads (center) with two real heads. Frank has already painted this cast bill.

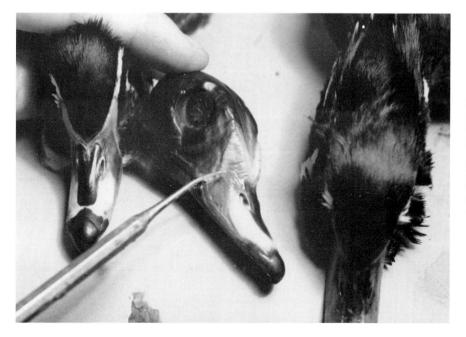

The cast heads are so accurate that they even have the wrinkles so commonly found on bills. They are also inexpensive, costing about ten dollars. The wood duck head and others are available through Wildlife Designer Series.

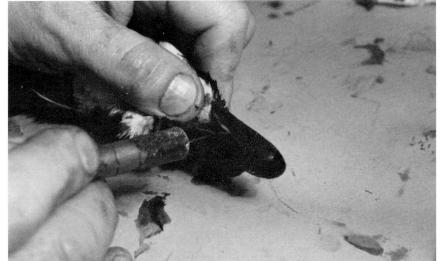

Separating the skin from the skull must begin on the lower mandible. An incision with the scalpel starts where the skin and feathers begin.

The next incision is at the beginning of the upper mandible. Note where the point of the scalpel is. The skin must be separated or disconnected from the upper mandible.

Frank peels the skin away from the upper mandible.

The skin that merges with the upper mandible is V-shaped. This flap must be entirely disconnected.

Pulling the V-shaped flap away from the skull.

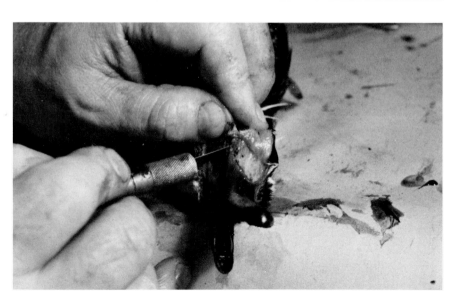

The skin must also be separated along the sides of the mandible.

More separating of the skin.

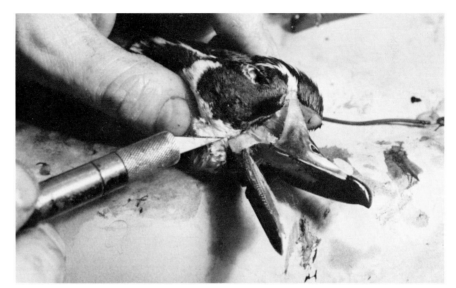

Progress so far.

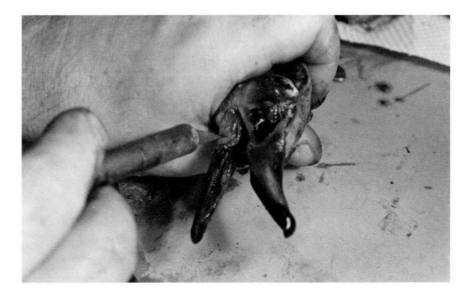

The skin pulled back from both the top and bottom of the skull.

Frank advises disconnecting the lower mandible by extracting one hinge at a time. In so doing he has reduced the size of the skull so that the skin is not ripped as it is pulled off.

Next the skin around the eyes must be severed. The small slit located below Frank's thumb is the eye opening. Note that Frank's little finger braces itself against the upper mandible.

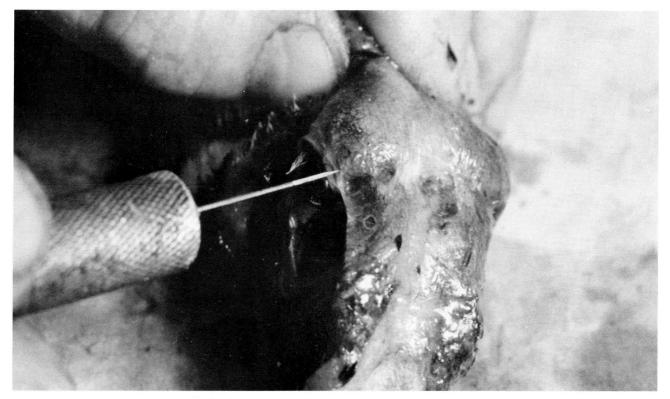

Pulling the skin back. Again, you must exercise caution when separating the skin from the flesh so that the skin does not tear.

Separating the skin from around the ear openings of the duck. These are located just behind the eyes.

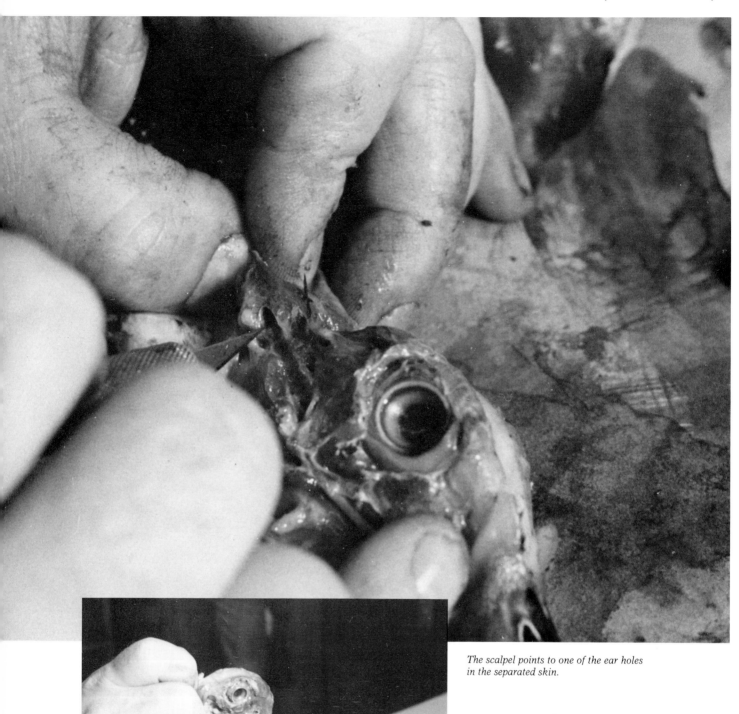

The scalpel points to one of the ear holes in the separated skin.

This picture shows the head skin pulled down to the base of the skull. Note the openings in the skull, which show where the eyes and ears are located.

Frank next holds the neck skin with one hand and pulls the head with the other.

Between Frank's hands is fatty tissue. This step finally separates skin and skull.

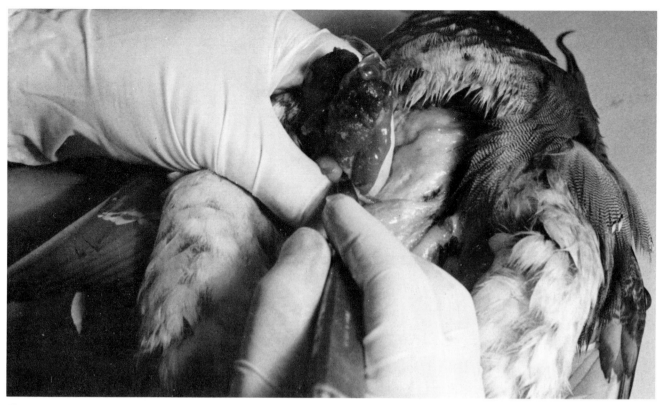

You must now return to the wing bones to remove flesh or meat from the bones. The humerus bone must be exposed and skinned out with the scalpel. This is the bone that was separated from the carcass.

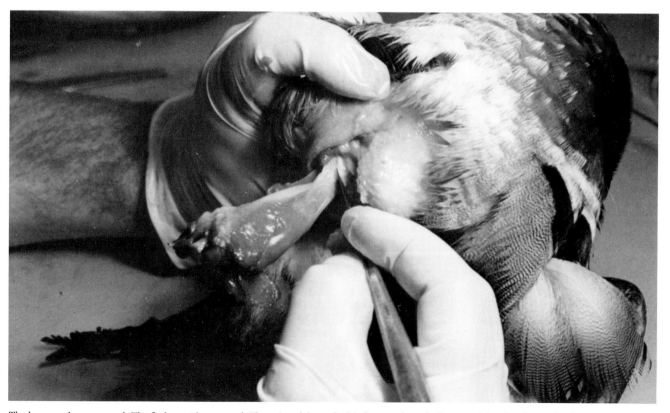

The humerus bone exposed. The flesh must be removed. The point of the scalpel indicates where the humerus joins the ulna and radius bones.

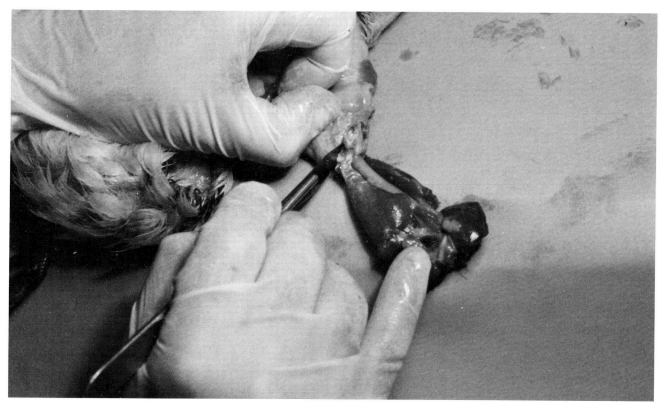

This photo shows Frank separating the skin from the joint. The skin in his left hand must be pulled down to expose the ulna and radius bones.

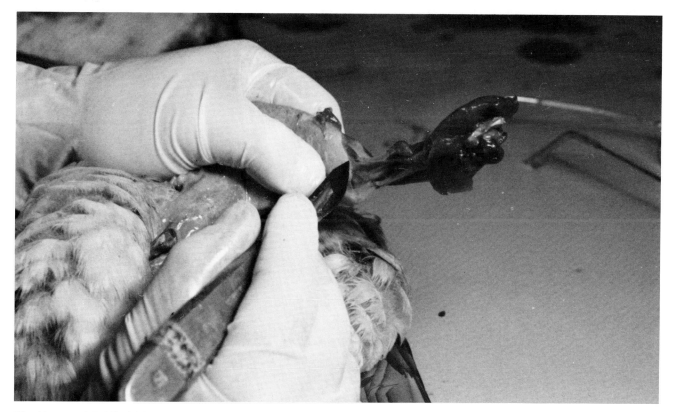

The skin separated at the joint.

*Frank then holds the ulna
and radius bones and with
the other hand pulls the skin
back so that it is inverted.*

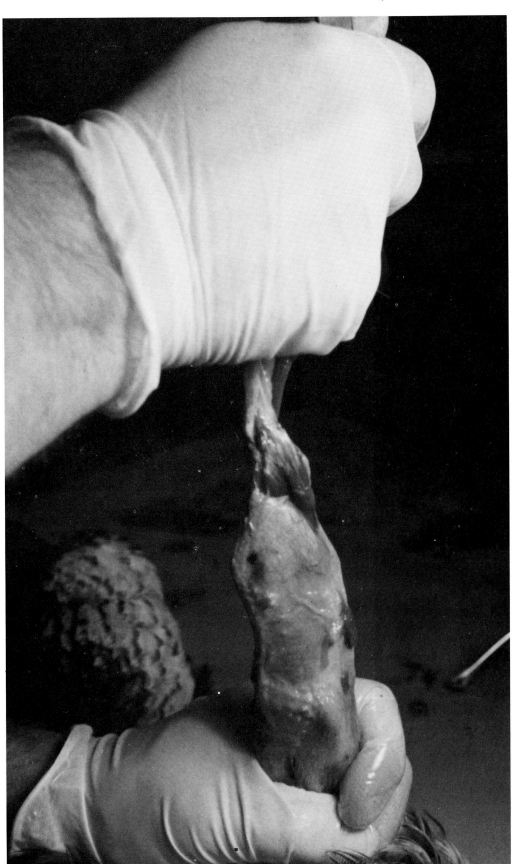

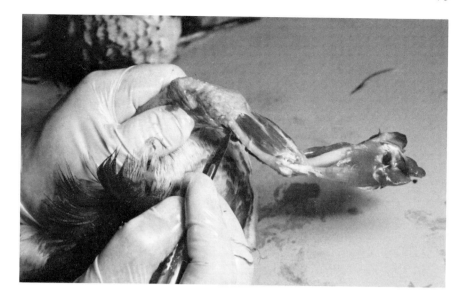

The other wing skinned back.

Flesh or meat must be removed from all wing bones that have been exposed.

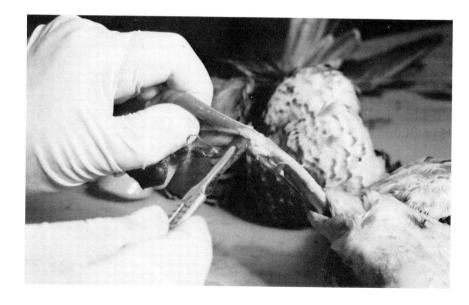

In this photo, you can see Frank removing flesh from the humerus bone. The ulna and radius bones have already been cleaned. Note how the flesh is sliced away with the scalpel.

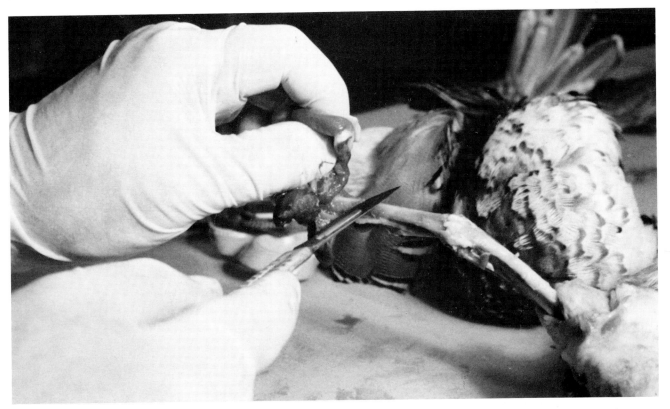

More slicing away of the flesh from the wing bones.

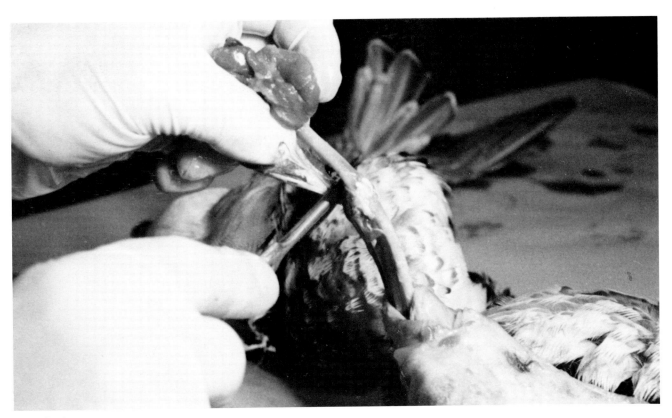

More cleaning.

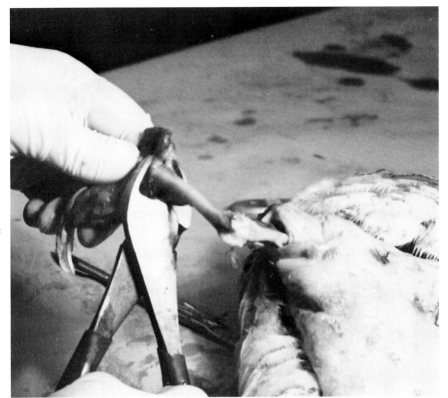

After the bones have been cleaned, the humerus knob can be removed. Leaving it in would cause the wing to stick out from the wrapped body or mannikin when it should lie flat. Wire cutters will do the trick here.

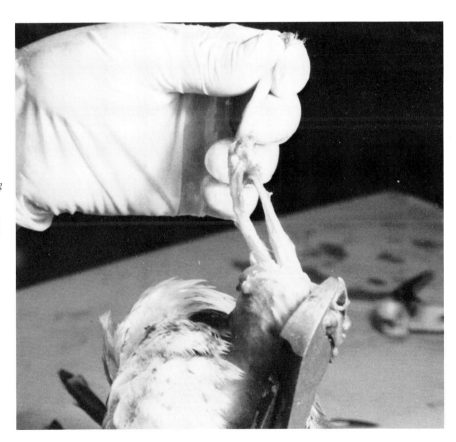

This photo shows the wing completely cleaned. The lower bones are the ulna and radius; the one Frank holds is the humerus. The humerus knob was where Frank has his thumb and forefinger.

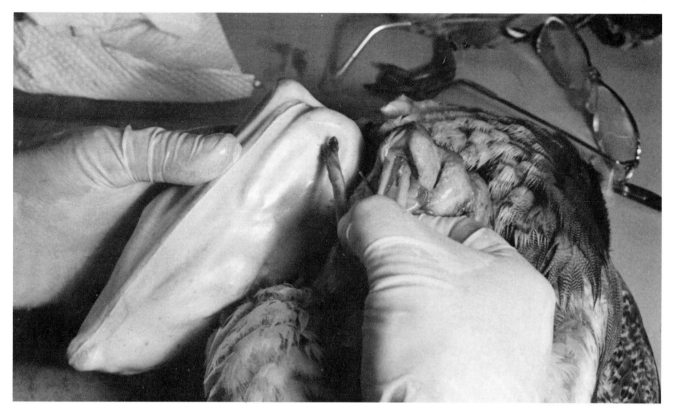

Frank demonstrates, using one of his mannikins, where the humerus bone will be located when the skin is placed over the cast body. Note that the humerus knob would have caused the bone to project incorrectly above the surface of the body.

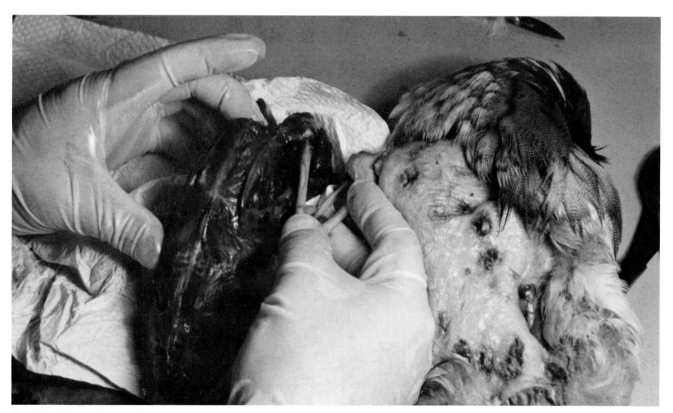

Here Frank shows where the humerus bone is located on the carcass.

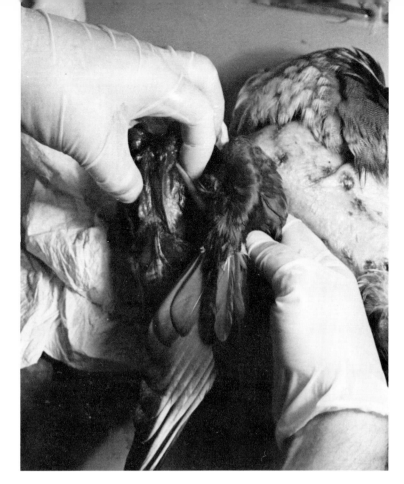

*In this photo Frank shows
how the wing folds when
it is in flight.*

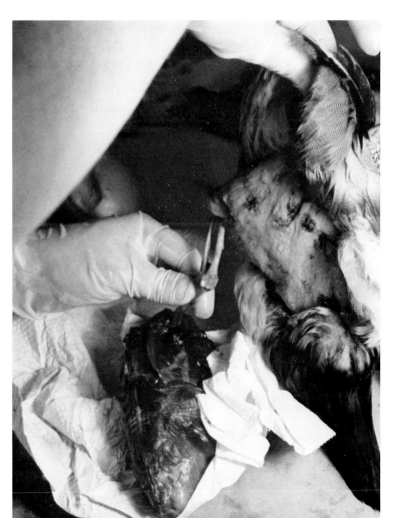

*Here Frank demonstrates
how the wing bones unfold
when in flight.*

The wing skin must now be inverted back to where it belongs on the cleaned bones by pulling carefully on the primaries.

as the other hand cuts it with the scalpel. Frank says that the taxidermist should "be sensitive" about doing this. Skin ripped here is not as easily repaired as the skin of the breast or a side pocket.

Frank advises disconnecting the lower mandible, removing with pliers the two hinges that hold it to the skull. Doing so reduces the size of the skull so that the skin can be pulled away with less chance of tearing.

If the taxidermist looks at the head of a duck, he will notice that the skin comes up the neck, travels over the bulge of the skull, and tapers in and around the bill. Were the size of the skull not reduced somewhat by removing one mandible, it would be very difficult to get the skin over the bulge of the skull without tearing it.

If the real skull is used, side cuts can be made on either side of the cheek or ear and down the side of the neck, but a seam may show, even with the best of stitching jobs. The best incision, according to Frank, is one along the throat. It should be made from the center of the lower mandible, and should be long enough to allow the skull to pass through the skin.

If an artificial head is to be used, some taxidermists will crush the skull so that it can pass more easily through the skin. Frank says that the hinges on the lower mandible should still be removed.

Other taxidermists recommend cleaning the skull while leaving it inside the skin. But Frank's method of cleaning, as described in chapter 4, is to treat the bird with various chemicals to remove fatty deposits and then tumble it in a dryer. Leaving the skull in the body while the bird is in the tumbler would tear feathers and damage the skin.

The taxidermist must continue to separate the skin from the skull by working from the corners of the jaws, then around the eyes and ear holes. A lot of care should be taken. The ears are severed and gently pulled free. After those areas are done, the skin can be pulled down to the base of the skull. Then the neck skin is held with one hand and the head with the other to separate the two.

Though the skull can be saved, Frank points out that it can never be adequately cleaned, and later on it will be subject to insect damage. But the biggest problem is with the bill, which can shrink, even with chemicals injected into it. And since it is fleshy, it, too, can be damaged by insects. For these reasons artificial heads, which include the bills, exist for many gamebirds. Through Wildlife Designer Series, Frank offers all North American waterfowl species of ducks plus castings for upland gamebirds, such as woodcocks, bobwhite quail, partridges, pheasants, turkeys, and

The wing skin must be pulled all the way. It is now no longer inverted.

quail. He also offers the glass eyes that the taxidermist will need regardless of whether the real skull or an artificial skull is used.

After the skin has been removed from the bird's body, the wings and legs need to be cleaned as well as the tail section, from which all flesh must be removed. The legs should be skinned down the tibia as far as possible – that is, to the heel of the tarsus – and trimmed of all flesh and tendons.

Next, the taxidermist cuts away the top of the tibia so that a stiff wire can be inserted into the center of the bone. Inserting the wire aids in the cleaning process and adds to the life of the mount.

The wings of the gamebird must definitely be cleaned. The taxidermist starts by exposing the humerus ball joint or knob. He uses two procedures. First, he trims all flesh from the humerus bone with the scalpel. Second, he cuts the flight tendon. This tendon attaches to the anterior portion of the ball joint and travels across the flight skin to the joint beneath the alula, or thumb. Opening the web will allow access to the ulna and radius for the cleaning. What Frank calls "skinning out the wing" begins by holding the humerus knob in one hand and the wing skin in the other and pulling. As the taxidermist pulls, his fingers can feel the bumps where the tissue connects to the bones. These bumps are the ends of the secondaries. Pulling will invert the skin.

When the bones have been exposed, they are cleaned with the scalpel. All the meat must be cut or scraped away. The bones can be rubbed with powdered borax to remove any flesh left over.

Frank says that the wing bones must not be broken. Since they are hollow, they can break easily, and there are no castings for them. But if they do break, a wire or plastic tubing big enough to hold the bones can be used for repair.

After cleaning the bones, the taxidermist removes the humerus knob, which until now had helped with turning the wing skin inside out. This knob, were it left in the skin, would cause a bulge when the skin is put on a mannikin or wrapped body. On Frank's cast bodies the knob or joint is not visible, but it is part of the overall shape of the body.

The cleaned wing, Frank says, provides a good opportunity to see how the wing unfolds for flight and how it closes up next to the body.

The final step is to invert the wing skin back to where it was originally. The taxidermist holds the primaries and gently pulls them back around the ulna and radius bones and the humerus bone.

He is now ready to degrease the skin.

4

Cleaning the Skin

Cleaning the skin basically means degreasing it. Fat deposits adhere to the skin as it is removed, and these deposits have to be eliminated. If the fatty tissues are not removed, the oil in them will yellow the feathers, causing "grease burns." As Frank explains, grease sends protein through the hollow shafts of the feathers and will turn them yellow, especially on the white breast, within a month or two. Grease also invites bacteria.

Taxidermists have traditionally used a wire wheel attached to a motor to clean a skin. It would seem a useful tool, but it can overclean the skin. If the taxidermist is not careful, he can get the skin so thin that it will fall apart when it is put into the sawdust-filled dryer described later. And if too much pressure is applied to the skin as it moves over the wheel, the wheel will tear the skin.

If the wheel must be used, Frank advises to begin the degreasing process at the tail and work toward the head. Working with the feather tracts instead of against them will result in fewer tears. One hand should be held under the skin to develop a feel for how much pressure is needed. And the taxidermist must hold onto the skin firmly or the wire wheel will grab it and pull it out of the taxidermist's hands.

If a wire wheel is not used, the alternative method is not difficult: it involves using a pair of scissors to cut away the fat. Frank says to press the scissors against the skin and go between the feather tracts. But the taxidermist must be careful not to cut the shafts.

There can be a tendency to get the skin almost paper-thin, like rice paper, in which case the feathers may fall out. Should this happen to a few feathers, Elmer's Glue can be used to put them back into place. Taxidermists can also get the head skin and the tail too thin, whereupon those feathers will definitely fall out. Frank advises working the areas with extreme caution.

Using the scissors is a time-consuming process because it means pinching the fat away. It should be done slowly and carefully to keep the skin and feathers intact.

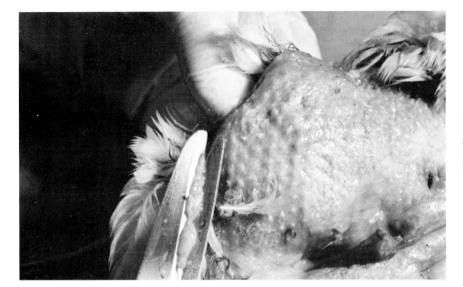

The next step in taxidermy is to clean the skin, or remove the fatty tissue. Frank calls this process degreasing the bird. The best tool to use is a pair of scissors. Frank advises pressing the scissors against the skin. Another tool is a wire wheel mounted on a motor.

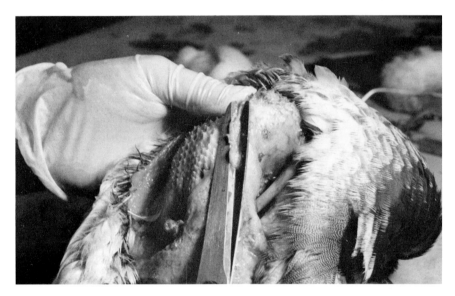

Degreasing also means getting the oil out of the inside of the skin. If the oil is not all removed, grease burns will occur, turning the feathers yellow. Note how close Frank shears away the fat. On the left of the scissors is the degreased area. The pointy bumps are where the feather shafts enter the skin.

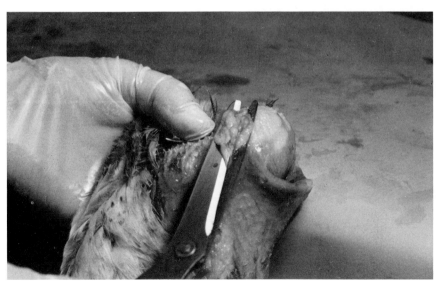

Frank pushes the skin into the scissors so that he can pinch it off. This is a time-consuming process but absolutely necessary.

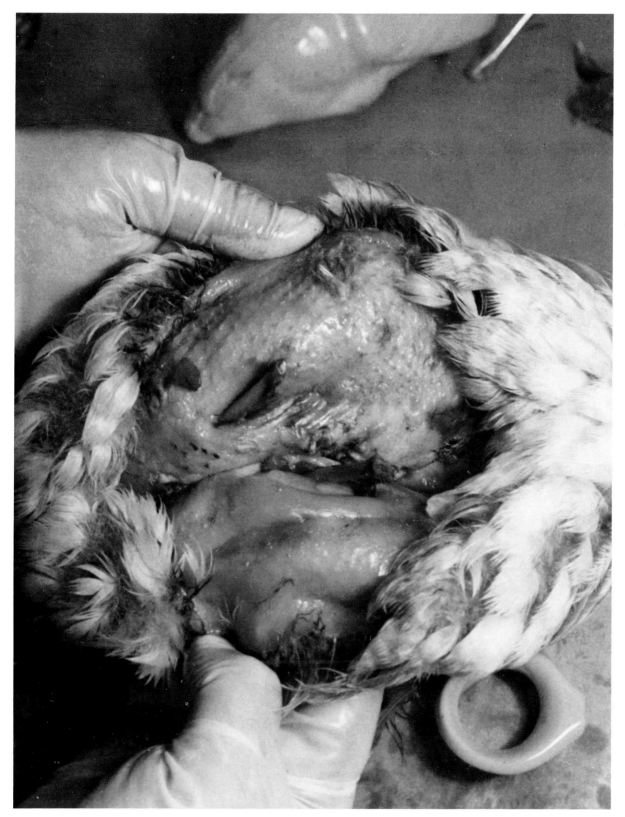

Note how much fat is on the skin after it has been removed. Compare the right side with the degreased left side.

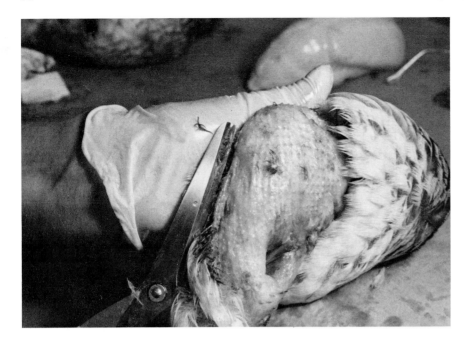

Meticulous care must be taken in removing the fatty tissue. Frank cuts away fat at the ventral incision, where the skinning process began.

Working on the head. The taxidermist must be careful not to get the skin too thin. If he does, the skin will end up with holes in it that will be difficult to repair.

One area not covered in the photos is the skull. Frank uses the artificial skull for his taxidermy work, and if he does not have one available, he casts one using the real skull and pouring a rubber mold. The casting is much more durable and easier to work with during later steps. But if the taxidermist prefers to use the actual skull of the bird, he must remove it from the skin and deal with it separately. First it must be thoroughly cleaned from the inside out. A small hole can be cut at the base of the skull to remove the brain, using either a hooked wire or a scraper. The taxidermist should then use powdered borax to absorb fluid and aid with the cleaning. All fluids and brain matter must be removed, the outside of the skull cleaned, and the eyes and flesh removed, with borax absorbing the fluids. And all flesh on the outside must be thoroughly removed before the skin is reattached to it. Frank says that this procedure takes a lot of time, as does sewing up the neck incision.

Degreasing with scissors is really half the process involved in cleaning the skin. The next step is to wash it well, using some easily obtained chemicals.

Large plastic buckets will be helpful here. The skin is first submerged fully in detergent and water. Frank recommends Dawn dish-washing detergent and warm water. Hot water might set some of the stains on the feathers.

The skin is slowly agitated in the solution and left to soak. Soaking begins to remove blood stains and grease that have inevitably gotten on the feathers. If a few feathers come off during the process, they can be reattached later using Elmer's Glue on the ends of the shafts.

Generally ten minutes of soaking time is enough. Soaking the skin for hours will loosen feathers within their tracts and soften the skin. And excessive moisture might encourage bacteria, which will eat away the skin after it is mounted.

The skin should be squeezed out gently and rinsed in cool water. The taxidermist should then look for what is called adherent coloration. This is the accumulation of unnatural colors that have been caused by anything from berries to minerals in the water the bird bathes in. To eliminate the colors, Frank recommends a product called Whinks, which has a small percentage of hydrofluoric acid and can be squirted onto the stains. They should disappear within minutes.

Inevitably some fat will remain on the inside of the skin. Frank suggests using a product called True-Tan

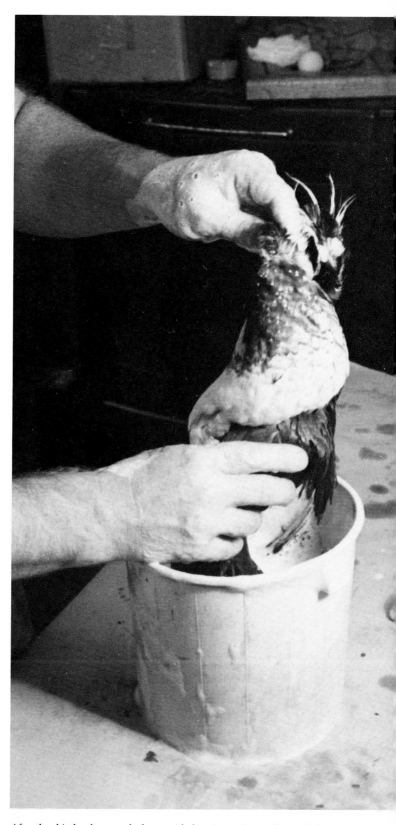

After the skin has been worked over with the scissors, it must be washed well. Make sure the bird is submerged. Frank advises a mild detergent and warm, not hot, water. He recommends using Dawn dish-washing detergent.

There will invariably be blood clots at the base of the feathers. Remove them with a soft toothbrush and some light scrubbing.

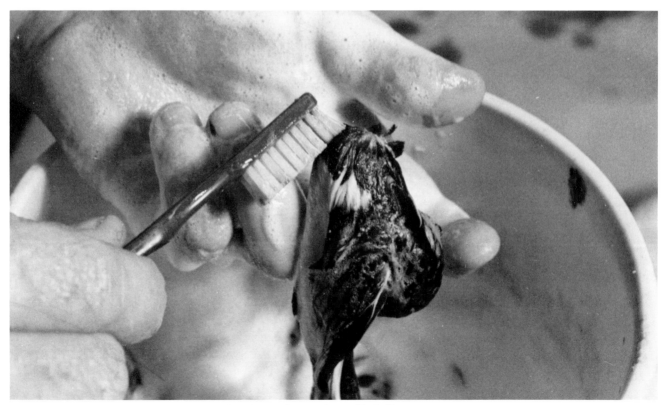

Frank advises looking for shiny spots of dried blood on the skin that must be scrubbed off.

The skin should be gently squeezed out and rinsed in water. Frank says that feathers will be lost during the washing and rinsing, but major feathers can be reattached with Elmer's Glue.

Grease Buster, available through Wildlife Designer Series. A solution of one tablespoon per gallon of water is made up in a bucket, and the bird is allowed to soak for twenty minutes. It is then rinsed in water. Other chemicals that will work are mineral spirits or white gas.

The final treatment is to use another Wildlife Designer Series product called Solvent Degreaser. It comes in liquid form and should be poured directly onto the skin, which is soaked for twenty minutes. The solvent will leave the skin extremely clean because it acts like a sponge to remove grease.

Frank warns against putting the skin down on newspaper during any of the washing operations. Newsprint will come off on the feathers and is almost impossible to remove.

The next stage of the cleaning process is drying the skin. This can be done in a secondhand dryer partially filled with sawdust. Sawdust, Frank says, will cause the feathers to fluff up as well as absorb liquids. Frank recommends using a hardwood sawdust because it will have less moisture in it than a softwood sawdust, like pine. Moisture ruins the absorption quality, and the sawdust is needed to get the feathers dry.

The vent of the dryer must be sealed off so that the sawdust does not escape. Plywood and fiberglass will bond the wood to the metal. Also, the heating elements must be disconnected, since heat is not necessary and would only harm the feathers.

The skin is tumbled for ten minutes and removed. The taxidermist will see a remarkable transformation in the skin. It will actually look fluffy.

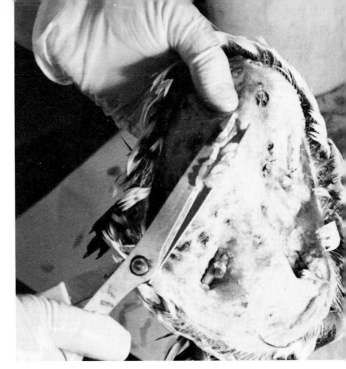

Next look for any fat that was not removed during the degreasing. Use the same method of pinching it off with scissors.

After washing and rinsing the skin, you may see what is called adherent coloration on the skin: anything that is not natural to the bird's coloring. It might be caused by food in the bird's diet, such as berry stains, or minerals in the water. Frank uses Whinks, which is ten percent hydrofluoric acid. He says to squirt it right on the adherent coloration. The unwanted stains will disappear, and the skin can then be rinsed with cool water.

The final stage is to dry the skin and remove the sawdust, which will have gotten into all the feathers, including the barbs and especially the down feathers.

When drying the skin, a hot-air appliance should not be used. It will curl the ends of the feathers, leaving a very undesirable look. A vacuum cleaner with reverse air will work nicely, as will an airbrush attached to a compressor. But the air pressure should be kept low. A great flow of air is not needed to remove the sawdust.

The taxidermist should take his time to get all the sawdust out. The flight feathers, wings, and tail feathers will dry first. The contour feathers will dry next, and the down feathers will dry last because they are nearest the skin. When the down feathers are dry, they will make the bird appear very fluffy.

As he is drying the feathers the taxidermist should not get the inside of the skin too dry. It must remain not only pliable for the mounting but also slightly moist so that it will shrink in place around the mannikin or wrapped body. In fact, one area in particular should be kept as moist as possible: the eyelids. As soon as the skin is blow-dried, moist cotton should be stuffed into the openings to keep them pliable when setting the glass eyes. When the skin does dry, it will conform nicely there. Similar precautions should be taken where the skin attaches to the bill.

Any remaining fat cells on the skin can be removed with True-Tan Grease Buster, a product available through Wildlife Designer Series. Frank recommends using one tablespoon of this chemical for every gallon of water. The skin is soaked for twenty minutes.

After twenty minutes, the skin is removed from the bucket and gently squeezed out. Plastic gloves are recommended.

The final step in the washing and degreasing process is to use another product available through Frank called Degreaser. Pour the liquid directly on the skin and soak it for twenty minutes.

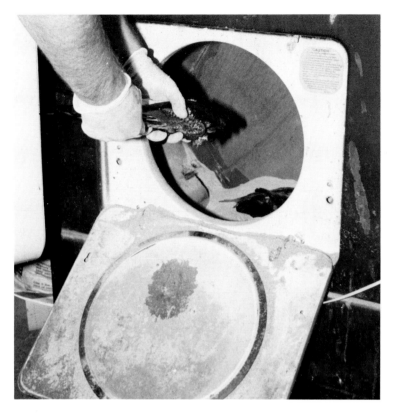

The best way to dry the bird skin is to put it into a dryer. Do not use a household appliance because you must put sawdust in it. A secondhand dryer should be purchased, and the vent can be closed with fiberglass and a piece of three-eighth-inch-thick plywood. Also, the heating elements must be disconnected.

Tumbling should not exceed ten minutes, at which time the skin can be removed.

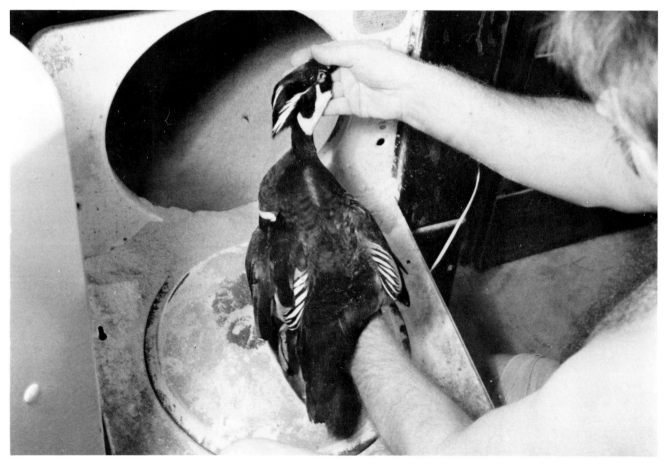

Frank fills the dryer with one-third sawdust. Frank points out that too much sawdust will crush or bend the primaries. Note, despite the sawdust on the feathers, how "lively" the skin looks after being in the dryer.

The sawdust will make its way into all the feather groups and tracts. The best way to remove it is with a vacuum cleaner with reverse air. Frank uses a secondhand Hoover vacuum cleaner.

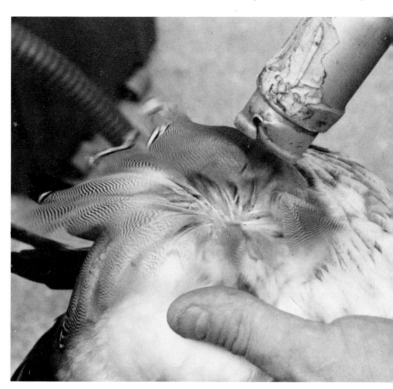

All the sawdust must be removed from the feathers.

An appliance that emits hot air should Frank says that heat will curl the feathe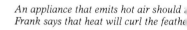

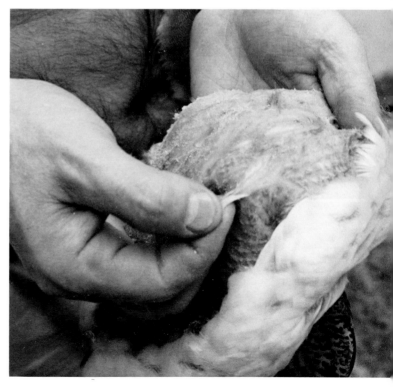

In this photo Frank blows dust out of the covert feathers. Sawdust will get trapped in the barbules. An airbrush can also be used to clean out the dust.

Getting at the down feathers, which must be especially dry. These are the feathers that give the bird a soft and full look. If they are not dry, they will not fluff out.

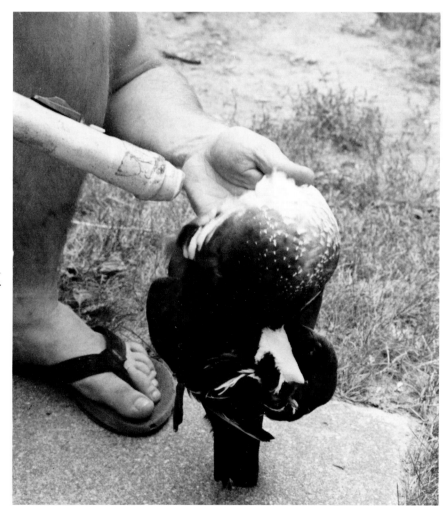

Oldsquaw landing.

Four oldsquaws.

Salmon-crested cockatoo.

Cygnet swan.

Wood duck.

"Ching Poot Bay." Harlequin ducks.

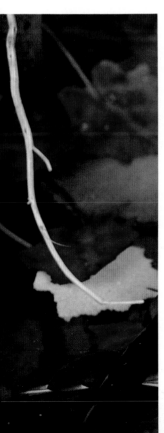

"Ching Poot Bay." Another view.

"Inciting." Redhead pair.

"Only for a Moment." Three oldsquaws.

"Down by the Brook." Hooded merganser pair.

"Low Tide." White-winged scoters.

"Nelson Lagoon." Steller's eiders trio.

Wood duck hen.

"On the Rocks." Barrow's and
common goldeneyes.

Woodcock.

Blue grouse. A table piece.

"Equinox." Greater scaup pair.

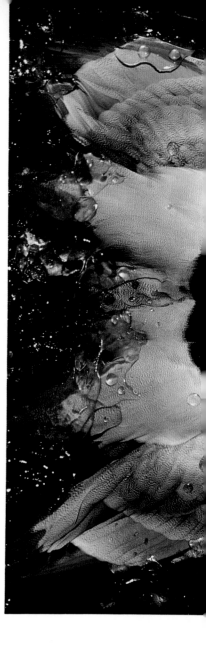

Wood duck pair.
Contemporary piece.

Wood duck pair.
Corner table
composition.

"The Robber." Canvasback and wigeon.

Three black ducks.

Gadwalls.

Cygnet swan.

"Master of Masters."

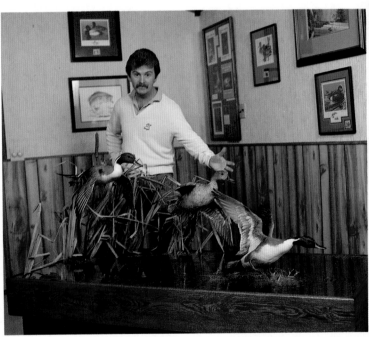

"After Hours." Three pintails.

"Autumn Retreat." Wood ducks.

Pintail. Executive Case.

"Politics." Eider and crows.

Ruffed grouse.

Woodcock.

Sharp-tailed grouse.

"Marsh Maestro."

A salute to North American teal.

Wood duck.

"The Lookout." Mandarin pair.

Dead game mounts.
A tribute to a
national heritage.

Spectacled eider.

Mandarin. Executive Case.

"Uprising." A bronze.

5

Mounting

It is difficult for the beginning taxidermist, and even many experienced ones, to mount a specimen without visual aids. It is even more difficult to mount one while looking at a live bird and attempting to understand what the various muscles are doing under all those feathers.

What, then, makes a good reference? Taxidermists will often use photographs of the live bird. But photos may not be enough. Frank makes two suggestions. One is to totally pluck an unmounted specimen. The taxidermist should pluck the bird carefully from head to tail, taking care not to tear or rip the skin. This study specimen can be kept refrigerated or frozen or, before freezing, molded into various positions. Through constant cross-reference with the specimen, the taxidermist can gain a better understanding of the overall muscle structure of the wings, legs, neck, and tail. He can eliminate, for example, the guesswork as to the size of wing muscles on the humerus or lower leg muscles on the tibia. In addition, he can note the points of insertion for wiring the wings of a bird in flight.

Another technique Frank recommends is to totally skin a specimen not to be mounted. The taxidermist should leave the head, wings, legs, and tail attached, allowing him to see firsthand the muscles and how they relate to each other. Head anatomy, facial muscles, and the neck can be studied. The taxidermist will find, for instance, that the throat and windpipe lie below the neck itself, creating an oval rather than a round shape. He can also study the points of attachment of the wings and legs as well as the caudal section.

Frank says that there are some areas of concern when skinning a bird. One is to not cut off the end of the caudal section. It must be left attached to the carcass for accurate body sketches. If the tailbone is left attached to the skin, the body measurements will be incorrect, and the remaining body will be too short.

Two other problem areas are the wings and legs. The previous chapter described how the wings are separated from the body and the ball of the humerus

This and the following photos offer an overview of a bird's carcass and show how the mannikin compares with it. This photo compares the Newmyer wood duck mannikin with two wood duck carcasses of different sizes. Frank says that he has made his casts to represent a medium-size bird.

bone is cut away. This ball joint must be created in the artificial body, so it has to be saved. If the ball of the humerus is discarded, the wing will end up being too short when attached to the body. The same holds true for the legs. If the tibia attachment is used, the taxidermist must record the length of the femur. But if the tibia is cut beneath the joint, the insertion point of the body will be lowered.

Finally, the taxidermist must realize when measuring the neck of a bird that it is the same length whether the bird is standing or flying. Only the position of the neck changes, which sometimes makes it seem longer or shorter. The neck of any bird is an extension of the back, not the shoulders or breast. When the major sections of the pelvis and back are fused and rigid, the neck becomes the most movable section of the upper back. The neck, with its flexibil-

ity, also accounts for much of the bird's balance and stance.

Insertion of the neck into the skull is very important. A bird's skull rotates freely on the axis vertebrae. It can move right, left, or up and down. The insertion point on a relaxed, standing bird will always be different from one on a flying bird. A study of the skinned or plucked bird will reveal the perfect neck-to-skull connection for any position or stance.

Frank makes some general statements about a bird's body as a way of summing up what the taxidermist should look for. All the muscles on the breast are extended wing muscles. They are compacted on each side of the sternum instead of on the wings. This compaction allows the wings to be light and bulk free. And all the muscles come together at the shoulders to work the wings. The back gives origin to the neck, which is

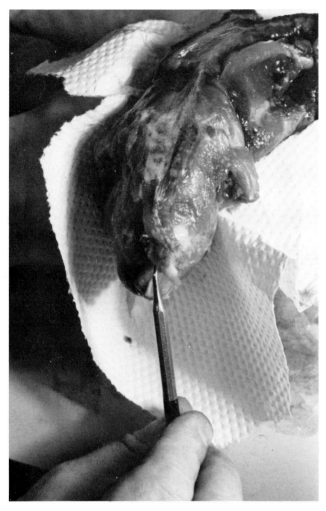

A carcass is worth studying, particularly if a molded mannikin is not available. Frank points out the clavical section, or shoulder blades, on the carcass.

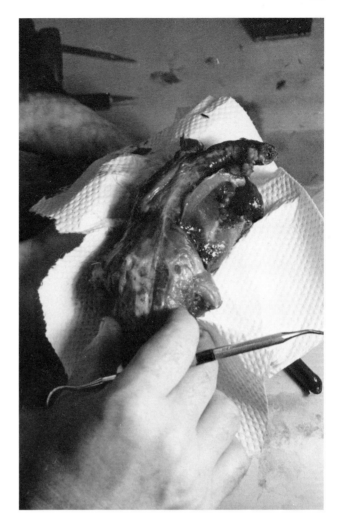

Here Frank shows how the back end of the bird pivots. It moves at the base of the shoulder blades.

placed between the shoulders. The wishbone creates a concave pocket beneath the neck. On the rear of the bird, the pelvis is stiff, yet the caudal section is able to rotate a full 360 degrees. The legs, starting at the femurs, are flat muscled, allowing for smoothness and sleekness; the tibia is more rounded. The breast recedes toward the rib cage enough to allow the jointed areas of the femurs and tibias to roll in and out while the bird is swimming or walking.

Any body-saving procedure, then, will offer excellent and original references for building the better bird body.

How does the taxidermist go about recreating the bird's interior? For many species of gamebirds, mannikins cast in a rigid foam can be obtained. Frank handles a line of mannikins for all North American waterfowl species and common upland gamebirds,

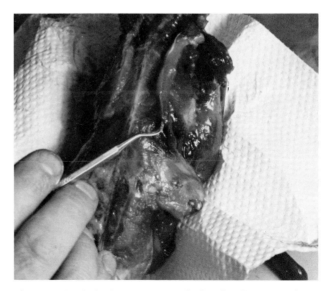

The pygostyle of a bird can also pivot. The dental probe points to it.

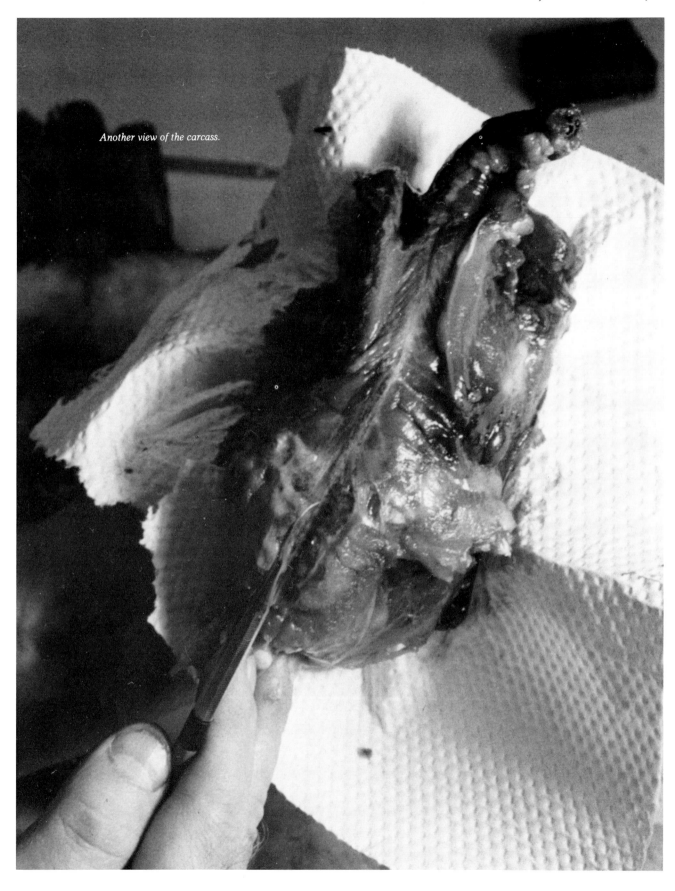

Another view of the carcass.

such as pheasants and quail. But the taxidermist may want to do a bird for which there is no mannikin. To make a body, the taxidermist should begin with sketches.

Drawings, though they do not offer three-dimensional views, provide good, permanent recordings of various body parts and the body itself. The taxidermist should make several drawings of the body showing the dorsal area, or top, the ventral area, or bottom, and side views. He can add various neck views. He must also take important body measurements and note the lengths and widths of the neck, humerus, femur, and caudal section. Additional sketches and measurements should be done on the clavicle width, the length and width of the scapula bones, the width of the pelvis at the femur, and the taper of the neck. And all the drawings should be labeled with type of bird, its sex and its age.

The taxidermist will find, when studying bird anatomies, that most waterfowl and gamebirds possess similarities that place each bird within a general family. These similarities will aid in understanding each bird better. Yet the taxidermist should avoid too many generalizations when mounting. Wood ducks and mallards are both ducks, but wood ducks don't act like mallards and vice versa. Ducks may have physical similarities, but they have definite differences in the way they relate to their environments.

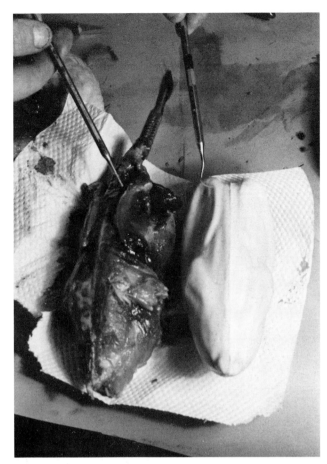

Comparing the mannikin with the carcass. Frank points to the clavicals on each.

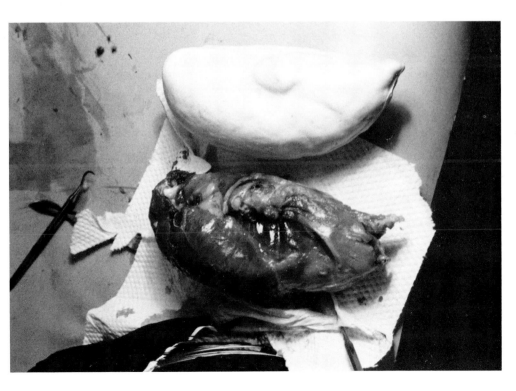

A profile view of the mannikin and carcass. Notice the definitions of anatomy on each.

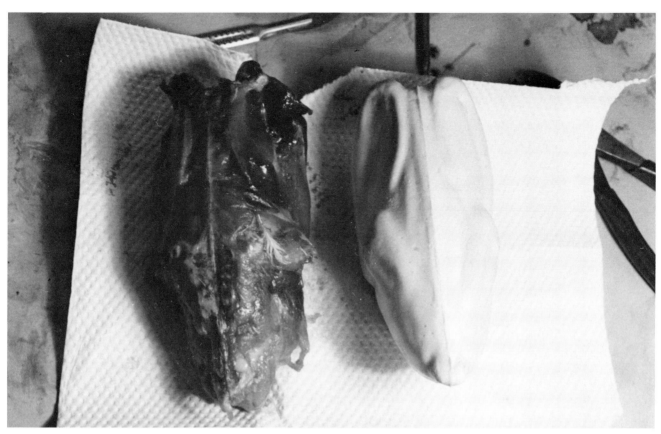

Though there are two pivot points on a duck's body, Frank's mannikin was created with a straight pose.

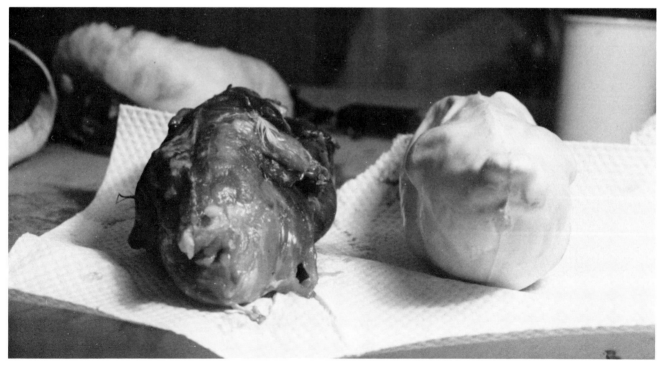

The rear of the mannikin and carcass. Frank points out that though there are different-size wood ducks, a medium-size body is acceptable for any because the skin, if left slightly moist, will shrink around the mannikin, and cotton filler can fill in the areas where fatty tissue has been removed.

This photo shows mannikin parts and duck parts. From left to right: mannikin, cast wood duck neck, cast foot, real foot, cast head, real neck and head, and carcass. The cast parts make up the Newmyer Designer Series System.

Before proceeding with the Newmyer system, Frank demonstrates the traditional method of wrapping a wildfowl body. Excelsior, also called wood wool, can be purchased from archery shops. This material is found in targets. Though Frank sizes the wood duck body by eye, it would be best to make patterns based on the carcass. You can do this by placing the carcass on its side and taking a side profile of it. You should also make a top profile, marking on it the shoulder blades, breast plates, and femur areas. The neck will have to be duplicated and can be made separately.

Frank says that wetting the excelsior will condense the body and make it more rigid. And some taxidermists apply shellac over the wrapped body. Yet Frank uses neither technique because any moisture inside of the skin can cause problems as the skin shrinks around the mannikin. He begins making the excelsior body by taking a four-ply string and wrapping it around the girth and length of the body.

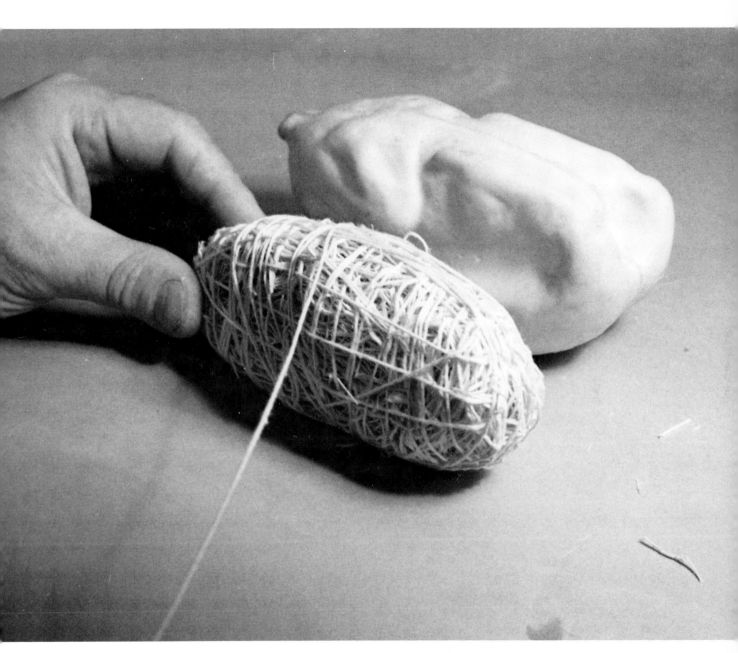

Note that Frank uses the string generously. He compares his wrapped body with his mannikin, though he could compare it with the carcass.

The shoulder blades are wrapped next. Frank made six-inch lengths of loose excelsior, also to be wrapped with string.

The shoulder blades must not only be wrapped but also bent in their middles. This is how they will look when attached to the body.

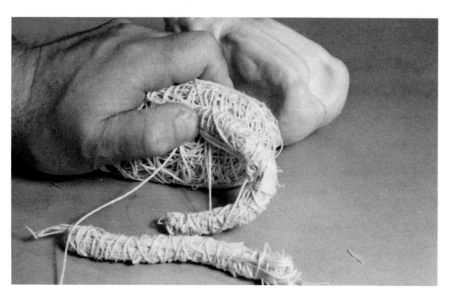

Locating them on the body. Note where they are on the mannikin.

This is how they are attached, with string holding them around the girth of the body.

These clumps of excelsior will be the breast plates for both sides of the body.

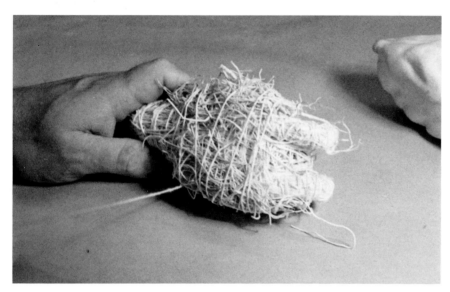

The breast plates are located on the upper sides of the body and to the rear of the shoulder blades. They, too, are attached with the four-ply string.

Frank has wrapped the shoulder blades in place, and he compares his wrapped body with the mannikin.

These clumps represent the femurs, which are located near the lower rear of the duck.

The wrapped femurs, the body, and the mannikin used as a reference.

The femurs in place. Frank says not to be afraid to move parts around or even press the body against a hard, flat surface to align or realign things.

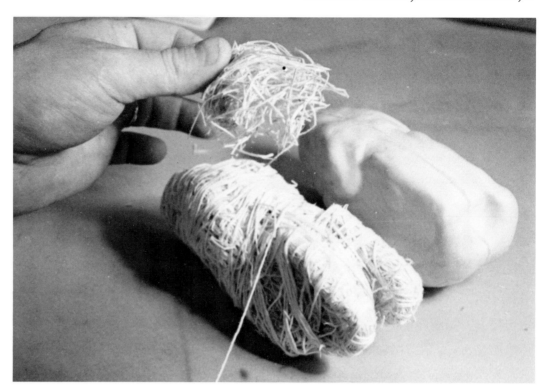

There is a high point on the body, located at the end of the shoulder blades. It is called the ilium. This clump represents that bone.

The high point in place. The added-on parts have flexibility and can be moved to some degree, as Frank does with one of the shoulder blades.

There are many materials and methods for making a bird body. The taxidermist can mold, carve, or wrap the body, to name a few of the methods used today. Some of the materials are wood, cork, Styrofoam, and urethane foam. The last material would seem to be the best, since it can be cut on a band saw and shaped with a knife.

When making a body, Frank prefers to use wood wool or excelsior and four- or six-ply cotton string. Excelsior is fine, curled shavings of wood that can be purchased from taxidermy supply stores or archery stores, where it is used for targets. Wrapped excelsior bodies are inexpensive and easy to make. Frank says that he can wrap a mallard body in about six minutes at a cost of about ten cents in materials. Another benefit of an excelsior body is that it will hold wires and pins that lock in the legs, tail, and wings.

When making an excelsior body, the taxidermist should go by the measurements and sketches taken off the real bird. Maintaining symmetry is most impor-

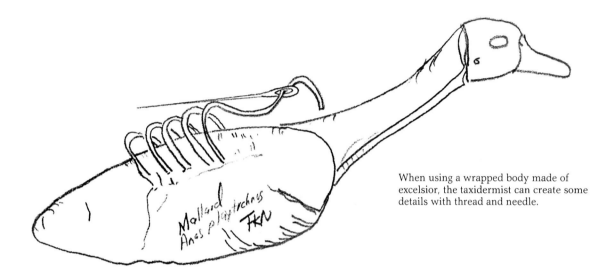

When using a wrapped body made of excelsior, the taxidermist can create some details with thread and needle.

The last step in making the body is wrapping it with tissue or toilet paper. This covering will prevent ends of wood wool from catching in the skin of the bird as it is taxied or moved on the body. The skin will slide more easily, and as it dries it will attach itself to the paper-wrapped body.

The tissue must be wrapped with string to keep it in place. The paper will absorb any fatty residue that might be on the skin. But, Frank says, no one can wrap a body that has the detail of one of his mannikins. Also, a wood duck mannikin only costs about five dollars.

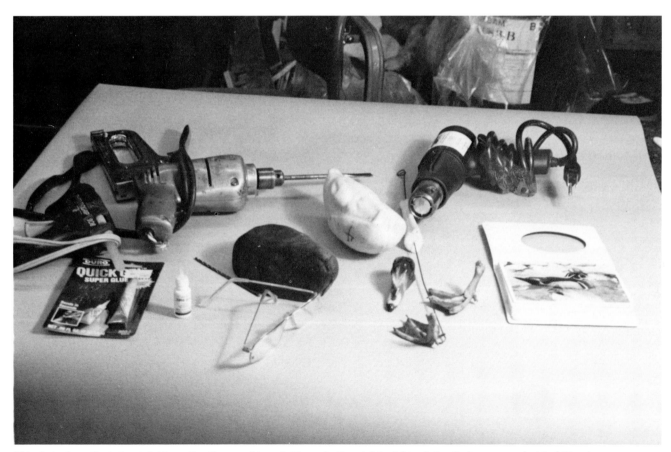

This photo shows the tools needed for getting the mannikin and skin ready. From left to right: a hot melt glue gun, an electric drill and one-half-inch spade bit, Quick Gel Super Glue, a one-eighth-inch twist drill, a Frank Newmyer cast rock, magnifying glasses, the artificial body parts, a paint stripping or heat gun, and the Mannikin Companion Photo Series *for a wood duck. The photo series is available from Wildlife Designer Series.*

This wood duck will be presented in a backwater habitat inside an Executive Case. The case is available through galleries or Frank's designer series. Here Frank starts to experiment with how the wood duck will look using the rock, carcass, feet, and neck. Note that the base of the case is recessed for a habitat display.

The Newmyer rock will, for this scene, give form to most of the mud bank. Here Frank positions the feet on the rock. For the basic wood duck stance, the distance between the legs will be about two and one-fourth to two and one-half inches apart.

tant. Calipers will help transfer the measurements.

The excelsior should be dampened for shaping and molding. To make a bird body, the taxidermist should start with an oval shape that looks like the sketches of the carcass. He then wraps it with a generous amount of string running around and along the length of the body. The calipers will be helpful here to compare the shape of the excelsior body with the sketches or real carcass.

After the excelsior carcass has been established, the shoulder blades are shaped, using elongated lengths of excelsior that are bound tight with string and attached to the body with more string.

Next are the breast plates, which are located on either side of the body to the rear of the shoulder blades. After they have been attached with string, the femurs are made from clumps of excelsior and attached with string. The final part is the neck. As has been pointed out, a bird's neck is not perfectly round because the esophagus and windpipe lie below the throat. An excelsior neck is attached using a wire run through the neck and into the body.

When putting together these body parts, the taxidermist can press, shape, and rearrange them slightly with his hands or even add material. This malleability is the advantage of using excelsior rather than rigid foam or wood.

After the body has been put together, Frank wraps it with facial tissue or toilet paper secured with string; the tissue prevents the excelsior ends from getting caught in the skin as it is placed around the body and moved into position. Also, the skin will actually attach itself to the tissue-wrapped body as it goes through its final drying.

When mounted, the wood duck will be in a backwater habitat scene, with all the components of that habitat made from artificial materials. Frank points out that taxidermists use too much organic material, such as real rocks, leaves, wood. Many of these materials, he says, will decompose, and rocks add too much weight.

Using a rigid foam rock, Frank positions the cast feet he will use instead of the real ones. These castings can be heated and bent to conform to the shape of the rock. The basic stance of the bird has now been established.

Though the excelsior body could be used for the wood duck project, Frank uses one of his mannikin line. The body is an anatomically accurate reproduction of a medium-size wood duck body. He also uses a cast neck. Frank calls his neck line Flex Necks. The artificial necks save several steps normally spent in constructing replacements. One important time-saving step is that the necks come with wires already

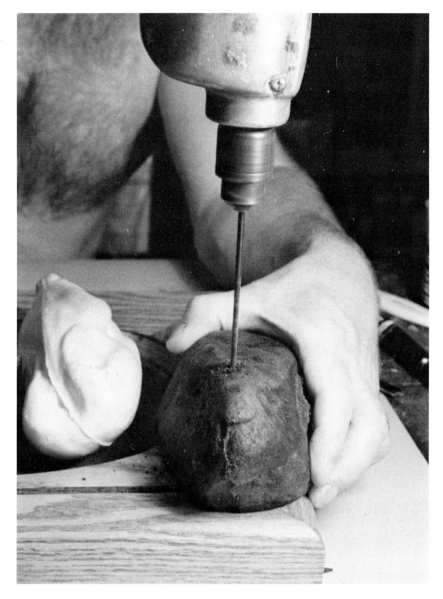

The Newmyer rock can easily be drilled to allow for the fourteen-gauge wires that will, in a later step, go through the feet.

installed along their lengths. When the base end of the wire is sharpened, it can be pushed into the mannikin or wrapped body.

The necks come in a variety of lengths and sizes. Ten sizes are available through Wildlife Designer Series.

FNN01. This is the largest of the necks, designed for use with larger ducks like canvasbacks, eiders, and small geese.

FNN02. For pintails and tree ducks.

FNN03. Designed for large ducks, such as mallards, redheads, and black ducks.

FNN04. A medium-size neck for ducks and pheasants as well as gadwalls, wigeons, and blue grouse.

FNN05. A small neck for small ducks, such as lesser scaups, shovelers, buffleheads, grouse, and Hungarian and chukar partridges.

FNN06. A wood duck size that also fits hooded mergansers and mandarins.

FNN07. The smallest of the necks, suitable for all teal and teal-size birds.

FNN08. A neck for Canada geese.

FNN09. A neck for medium-size geese, blue geese, and snow geese.

FNN10. A neck for a turkey.

The wire at the base of the neck is long enough that it can be run through the entire mannikin or wrapped body, looped over, and bent back into the body. This

The Newmyer artificial feet with predrilled holes for mounting wires. Made from rigid foam, they can be heated and bent so that they conform to the shape of the rock. The feet must be attached to the body before they are attached to the rock.

After being heated, the feet are flexible enough to be bent to fit the rock. Frank advises holding the feet in place for about forty seconds, enough time for them to take a new shape.

The next step is to attach the Newmyer artificial flexible neck to the body. The neck comes with a light-gauge wire that runs through it. The ends are looped so that the wire does not pierce your fingers. The loop at the base must be cut off; then that end of the wire must be pushed into the mannikin and out the rear of the body. You can use pliers to loop it over and bend it back into the body, which secures it permanently. Frank says to make sure that the neck is flush with the body.

procedure insures that the neck will not separate from the body. Hot melt glue will help secure an artificial neck to a cast body.

The next step is to get the skin ready to be put on the mannikin. Frank recommends using powdered borax, which will preserve the skin when the borax is rubbed into it and also lessen shrinkage somewhat. Frank does not suggest granulated borax for this purpose because it is too abrasive on the skin.

Frank uses a four-point locking system for properly placing the skin on the body. The body is placed in the skin so that the neck protrudes through the neck skin. But the first lock point, as Frank describes it, is at the pygostyle. The tail skin should be exactly centered on the tail and held in place by a long pin with a head large enough to make the pin easily maneuverable.

The next lock point takes care of the legs. Since the femurs were removed and will be replaced with artificial legs, only the tibias have to be locked in place. But first they have to be built up with clay and string because the muscles and flesh were removed during the cleaning operations. Then a sixteen-gauge wire is run up through the center of each tibia bone and inserted into the artificial body until it goes out the back, where it is bent over and clinched, or bent over and pushed, back into the body. This process will secure the tibias permanently. The taxidermist must make sure they are tight against the body. The locations for inserting the wires are marked on the Newmyer mannikins. Enough wire must protrude from the bottom of the tibia bones so that the artificial or real feet can be attached.

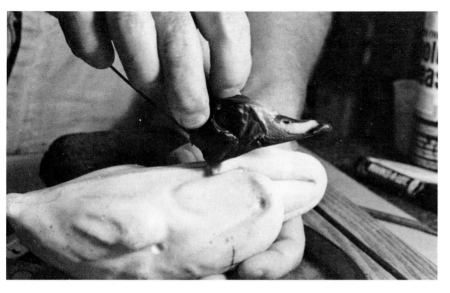

Birds' necks can take a number of positions that represent relaxed, semirelaxed, preening, or even threatened attitudes. Frank points out that when a duck is relaxed, its neck seems to disappear. The neck will conform to a **S** shape, with the upper portion of the neck resting on the body. That is the position in the photo. The rest of the neck is in the clavical opening.

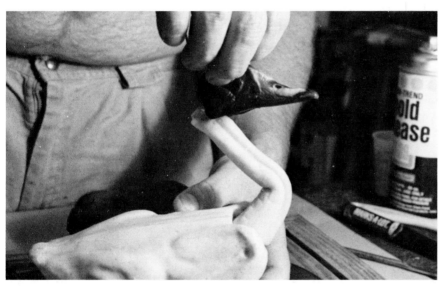

A bird can be mounted with a high neck, though this position would not make for a quiet, serene pose.

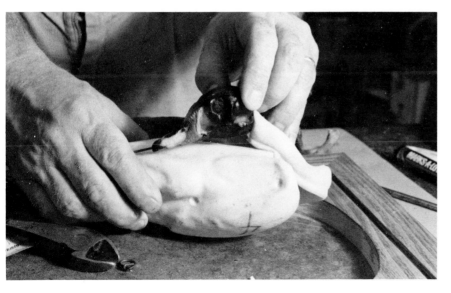

This is the neck position for a sleeping duck. Frank points out that no matter how one of his necks is bent, it will not break.

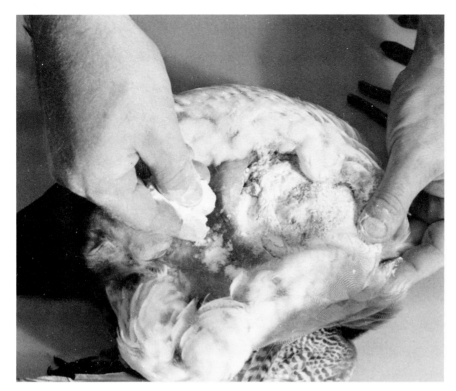

The skin must be readied for the insertion of the mannikin. The best preparation is to rub powdered borax right into the feather tracts. Granulated borax should not be used, since it is too coarse for the skin. Powdered borax can be purchased from almost any supplier of taxidermy equipment and chemicals.

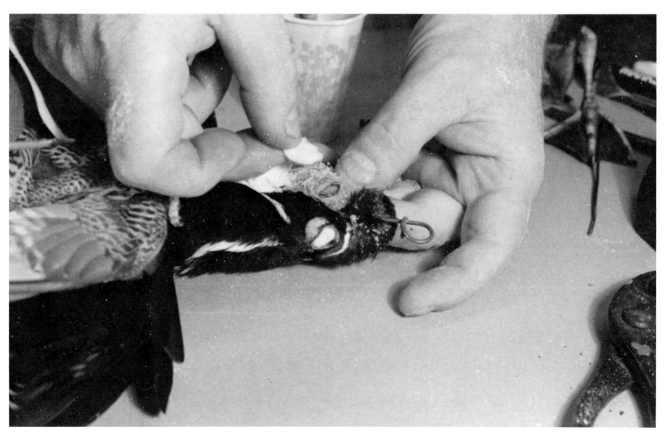

Another preparation is to put wet cotton on the inside of the eyelids to keep them moist. The openings must be slightly damp so that the eyelids do not dry out and become hard. If the feathers get wet from the cotton, they can be dried with lacquer thinner.

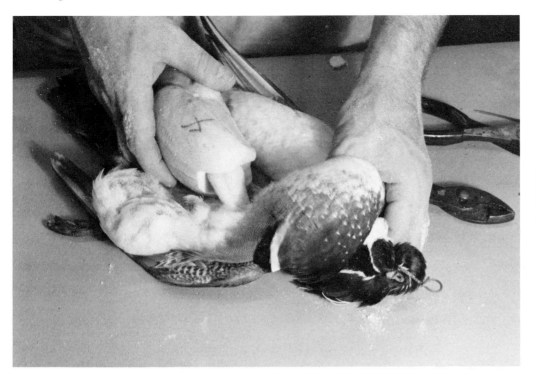

Inserting the mannikin into the skin. Note the neck wire that protrudes through the bill opening in the head.

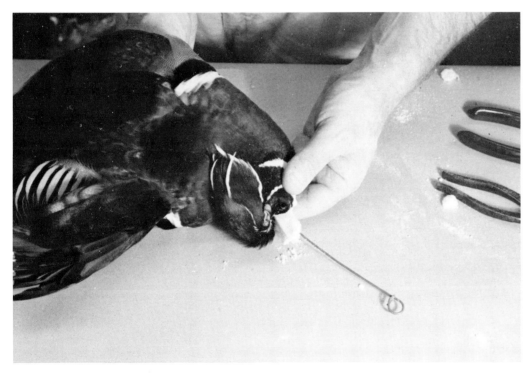

Frank has pulled the neck skin down around the artificial neck. This way no glue will get on the feathers when he is attaching the head to the neck.

Next, he pulls the skin down until it fits correctly around the pygostyle of the mannikin.

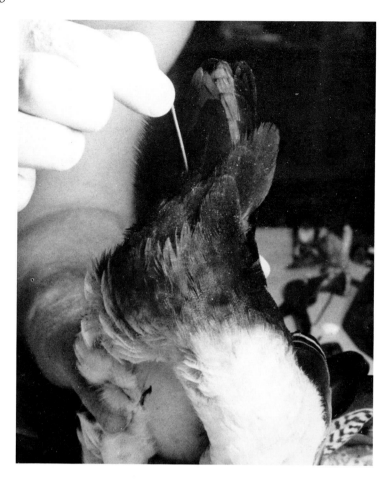

Frank has designed a foolproof
system involving what he calls
lock points. Using long pins, he
literally locks the skin in place
until it draws in around the
mannikin. In a somewhat damp
climate with temperatures
in the seventies, most of this
shrinkage will take place in
two days for a duck. His
mannikins are an ideal
substitute for the excelsior
bodies for two reasons. One,
the plastic holds the pins
better, and two, the lock
points are marked on the
mannikins. In this photo
Frank locks in the tail. He
can feel on the mannikin
where the lock point is; he
then runs the pin into it. On
the skin, this pin should be at
the center of the tail.

Other parts of the anatomy to
lock in place are the tibia bones,
which must be exposed through
the central incision on the skin.
Note that one sticks out next to
Frank's left hand. A light-gauge
wire is then run through the
center of each bone. One end of
the wire will be locked into
the mannikin and the other end
will be run through the cast feet.
Enough wire must be used so
that it will accommodate the
feet and still go through the
artificial rock, where it will
anchor the bird.

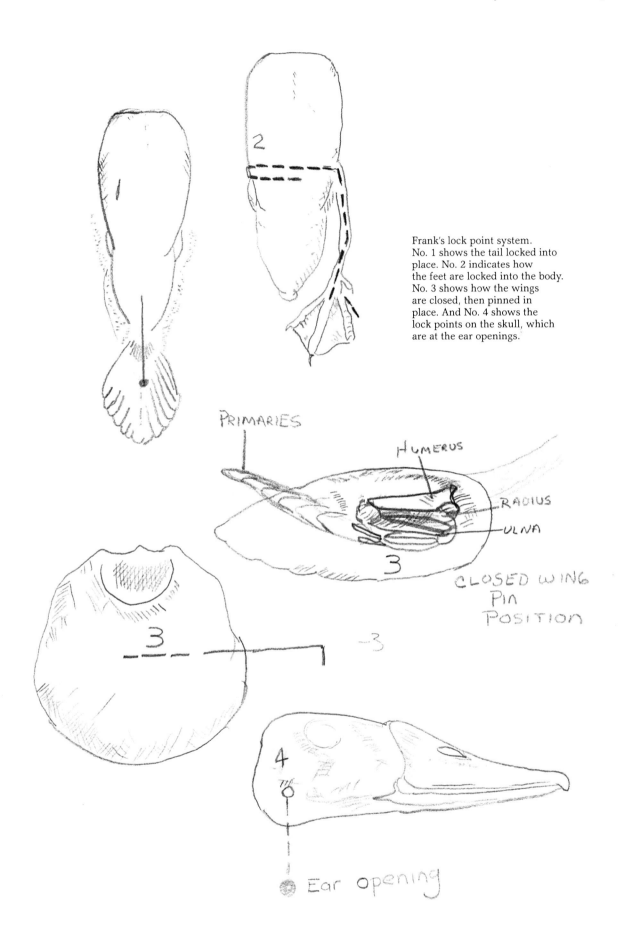

Frank's lock point system.
No. 1 shows the tail locked into
place. No. 2 indicates how
the feet are locked into the body.
No. 3 shows how the wings
are closed, then pinned in
place. And No. 4 shows the
lock points on the skull, which
are at the ear openings.

PRIMARIES

HUMERUS

RADIUS

ULNA

3

CLOSED WING
PIN
POSITION

Ear opening

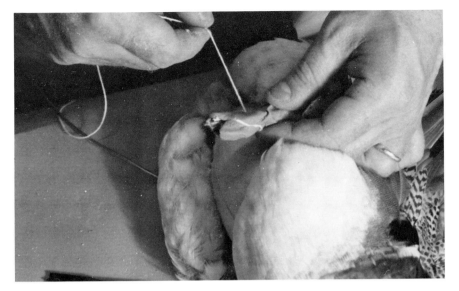

The tibia bones must be made bigger on their ends to recreate their original shape. This step can be done with clay, and the clay wrapped with four-ply string. The string will hold the clay in place.

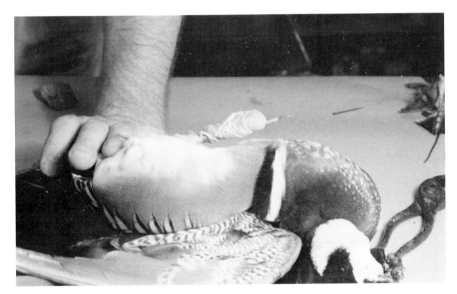

The tibia covered with clay and wrapped. Note the wire that is exposed at the end of the clay.

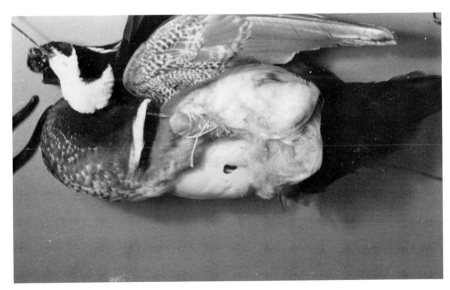

The tibia wires must be run into and through the mannikin so that they go up through the back. They are then bent over and pushed back into the plastic. Frank has used a Magic Marker to indicate where the lock point is for one of the feet. Note the excess wire that extends to the right of the photo.

Next, the wings are locked. A wire must be run through the ulna and radius to hold the wing bones in place.

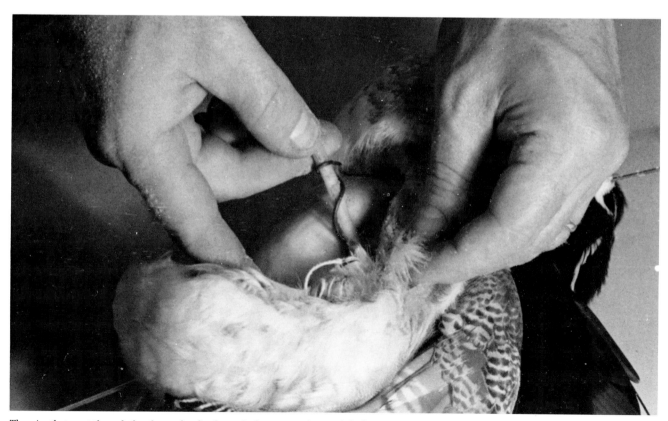

The wire that went through the ulna and radius bones is then wrapped around the humerus bone, with one sharpened end exposed.

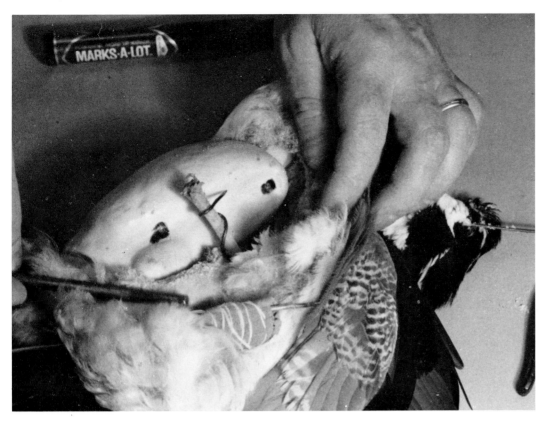

This photo shows two black marks, one for a foot wire, one for a wing. The mark to the right is where the humerus wire will be locked into the mannikin. These lock points can easily be found on the cast body, but they are not so easily seen in photographs.

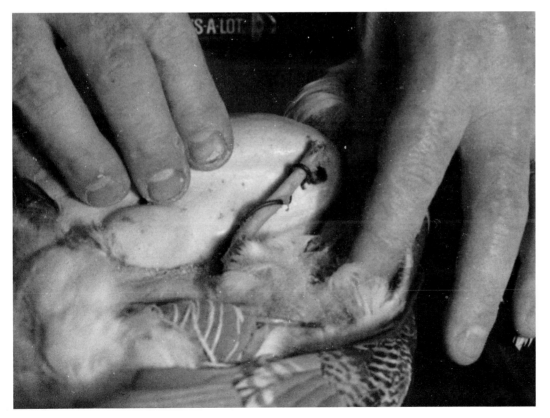

The humerus bone is locked in place. Frank reminds the taxidermist that if the humerus knob had not been removed, it would have pushed the wings off the body, making them look unnatural.

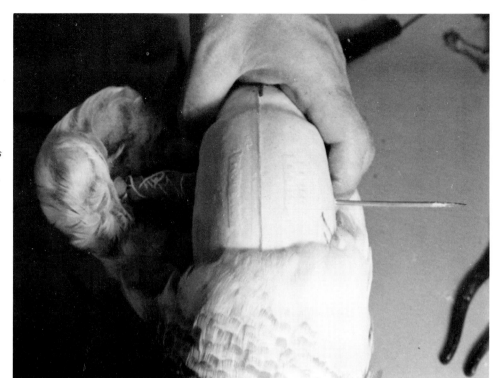

The wire that supports the tibia bone is run through the mannikin.

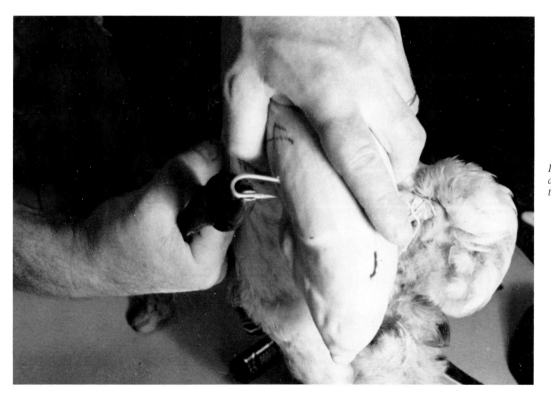

It is then looped over and pushed back into the body to lock it.

Frank advises folding the wing into as closed a position as possible before locking it in place.

While holding the wing slightly away from the body, Frank adjusts the skin of the side pocket so that it flows over the wing. If he did not do this, the skin would look pinched in.

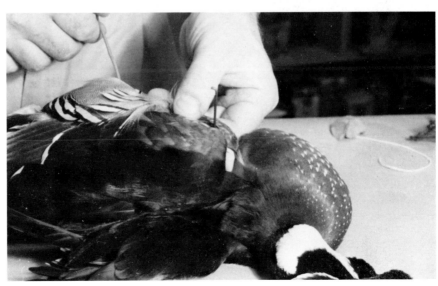

More adjusting of the side pocket so that it overlaps the wing slightly. The wire sticking out by Frank's thumb is the one that runs through the ulna and radius. Any wire sticking out will have to be cut or turned over and pushed back into the body.

Frank shows how the side pockets overlap the wings. This overlap is typical of a duck in a resting or relaxed position. After you feel comfortable with the positionings, lock them in place with pins. These can be removed later, or the heads can be clipped off with the shafts left in place.

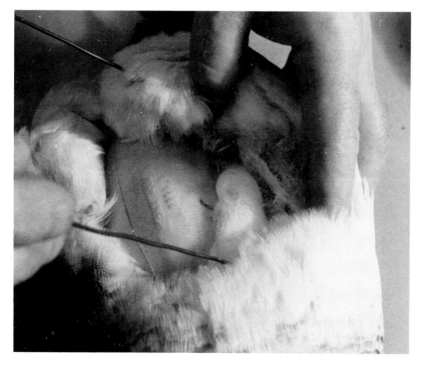

Because all the fatty tissue has been removed, the duck's skin is still much bigger than the mannikin in some places. To compensate, cotton must be added. Here Frank is filling the side pockets to simulate fatty tissue.

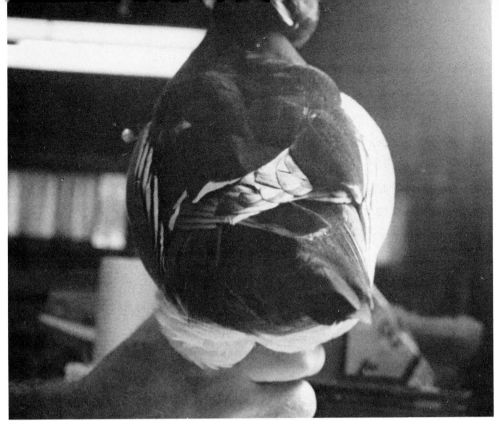

This photo shows the difference between the two side pockets. Cotton has been added to the right side.

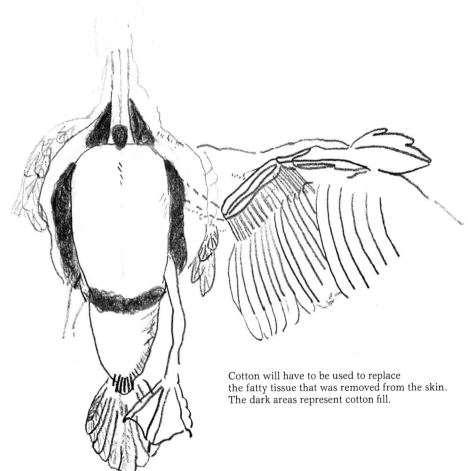

Cotton will have to be used to replace
the fatty tissue that was removed from the skin.
The dark areas represent cotton fill.

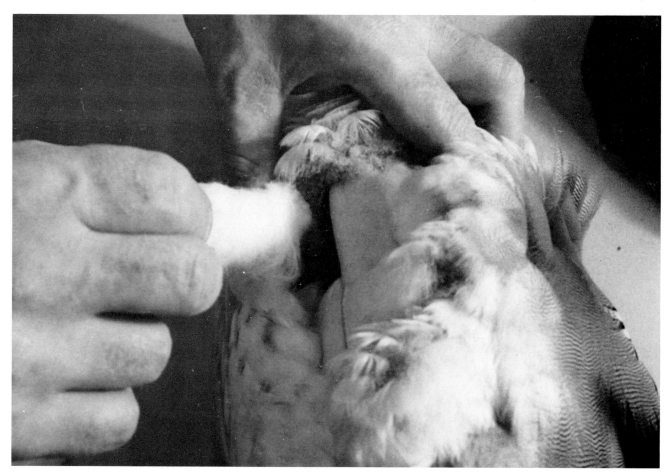

The bulge on the duck's neck is the crop. This area must be filled with cotton.

The next parts of the skin to be locked in place are the wings. It is the humerus bones that must be locked into the body. Pins could hold them, but Frank recommends using an eighteen-gauge wire that is run between the ulna and radius bones, wrapped around the humerus bones, and pushed into the body just inside the **C**-shaped bulge of the shoulder blades at the neck end of the body.

When both wings have been fastened securely in place, the taxidermist should check the accuracy of the wing length and placement. The primaries should be closed together to see how their tips line up, and their distance from the tail should be noted.

The side pockets have the highest concentration of fat of any place on the body. Since the fat was removed in the cleaning process, there will appear to be extra skin in that area. This skin must be filled before it is sewn together, and cotton is a good substitute for the missing fat. The flanks and the tail end of the bird should also be filled.

Frank says that it is very important to understand how feathers lie when taxiing the skin. Scapular feathers, for example, are a cover for the shoulders of the bird and form a perfect union with the side pocket feathers. They rarely stay high on the back, however, because the wings are bulk free. Wing bones in particular are hollow, with very little fat on the inside of the wing structure. In cold weather the bird's wings are protected by the scapular feathers. They are an insulating feather group.

The mantle feathers are the upper back feathers. They should never be pulled far up the neck. Nor should they be rolled over the scapulars.

When getting the wings placed properly, the taxidermist must fold and lift them within the side pocket feathers. The scapular feathers should, then, be able to flow smoothly down the shoulders and over the wings. When the wings have been placed correctly, with symmetry and balance, they are pinned to the body. Two pins can be used. One is pushed through the forward section of the wing at the joint of the digits and radius and ulna bones, and the other can be placed near the radius and ulna and humerus joint. These pins will hold a closed wing securely.

If the wings are to be open, they must be wired. To do so, insert a wire along the humerus in between the radius and ulna to the very end of the digits. Once this wire is placed correctly, it is wrapped tightly with string or thread against the humerus. Then the radius and ulna bones are wrapped with clay and string to replace what muscle was removed during the cleaning. The humerus is also built up with clay and string, and wire secures the humerus to the body.

If the bird is flying, there is no need to bring wire out of the feet. But the wire should be run from the inside of the skin down the tarsus and into the center toe if a real foot is used.

Many taxidermists make a simple presentation of a bird in flight. It involves nothing more than supporting the bird by a wire that is attached to the wall, in which case the supporting wire must be attached to the mannikin. It should be heavy enough so that it supports the weight of the bird. Frank recommends passing a sharpened end of the wire through the side feathers of the breast. The wire is placed on the wall side of the bird. It must go through the body and out the other side, but not out the skin. It is then clinched to create a supporting hook.

If a flying pose is chosen, or even a swimming one, some alterations should be made, especially on a cast body. Frank suggests grinding three-sixteenth to one-half inch off the breast of the bird, using a bench grinder. The breast takes on a flattened look when the bird is swimming or flying, actually dropping forward or flattening as it pushes forward in the water or air. The mass of the body, when meeting a mass of water or air, takes on the flatter, more buoyant appearance.

The fourth and final set of lock points are on the head. These locks will be described in the following chapter.

Progress so far. Note the pinhead in the side pocket.

6

Attaching Head and Feet

Before the head is attached and the skin around it locked in place, the bill should be painted. Frank has developed the *Mannikin Companion Photo Series* for his artificial heads. Each album contains twelve color photos of the head, body, and feet. A real bill should not be used. Colors will fade once a bird has died, and freezing will overemphasize certain colors on the bills and feet when they are allowed to dry out. Also, Frank says not to use a painting: the color transitions are too direct and not as blended as they should be on a bill.

Frank recommends using an airbrush for painting the bill and later the feet. The color transitions are not sharp on a wood duck bill; the airbrush will apply thin coats of different colors that will blend into each other. A typical airbrush set consists of a "brush," which looks like a hose nozzle with two tapered ends, a color cup, a hose, and a compressor.

There are paints made specifically for an airbrush, such as acrylics and some lacquers. The acrylics are thinned with water and the lacquers with lacquer thinner before they are put into the airbrush. But the needle in the head of the brush can clog easily, so it should be cleaned frequently with the appropriate paint thinner.

Bills have that fleshy look that is difficult to capture with brushed-on paints. It is the reason many carvers paint wooden bills with an airbrush. But if too much airbrushed paint is applied, the resulting look will be a ceramic one. The airbrush must be used sparingly, but it can create color transitions the way no other tool or brush can.

Why paint before the skin is mounted over the head? Paint that gets on feathers, even water-based paint like acrylics, is difficult to remove.

Frank advises the taxidermist to follow the colors on close-up photos of live birds. But rarely can a taxidermist find a photo of the underside of a bill. That is why his *Mannikin Companion Photo Series* will prove so useful. Whatever reference photos the taxidermist uses, he will find that the short bill of a wood duck has a black tip and ridge, white sides, and a red base bordered with a narrow yellow line.

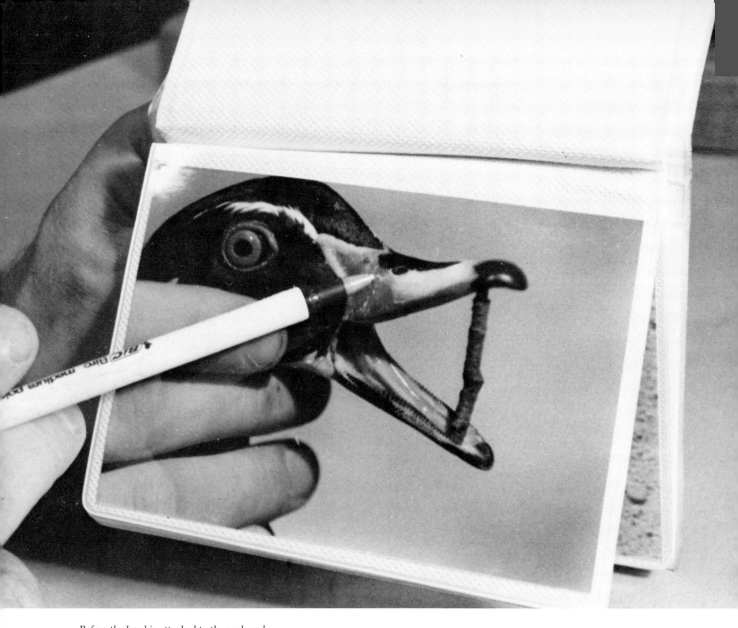

Before the head is attached to the neck and the skin is put in place, the bill must be painted. Taxidermists can study the artificial bills and feet in the Mannikin Companion Photo Series. He has one album for each of the twenty species of duck, and each album contains twelve photographs. In this photo Frank points to the various colors on the wood duck's upper mandible, showing that the different colors do not have sharp transitions but instead blend into each other. Frank suggests experimenting with different kinds of paints, though he will most often use acrylic lacquer colors. Red, yellow, black, and white are needed for the wood duck bill.

Feet are easier to paint since they do not have a variety of colors. But the scales on the feet may have to be emphasized. So a light coat of a dark color will have to be applied. This application can be done with a brush.

On Frank's artificial necks, the wire that protrudes through the top end of the neck must be curled into a loop. Doing so will keep it from impaling the skin and will aid in attaching the skull to the neck.

The next step is to take the artificial head and bore a half-inch-diameter hole in the back of the skull with a spade bit in an electric drill. The hollow skull is then filled three-quarters full with hot melt glue. Before the glue cools and gets hard, the looped neck wire is inserted into the hole in the back of the skull. The taxidermist must hold the head and neck in the proper position as the glue cools and locks the two together.

Frank uses a Pasche airbrush with a VL3 tip to apply the colors. To make the paint adhere better, he says, he first brushes shellac thinned with shellac thinner over the bill. The airbrush will spread the paint more evenly than a bristle brush will.

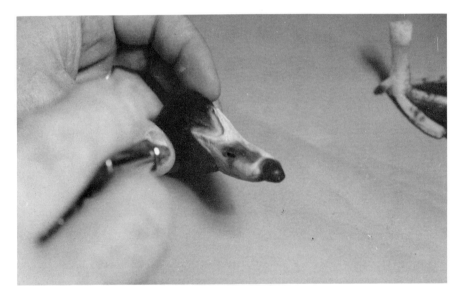

A light basecoat of white is needed.

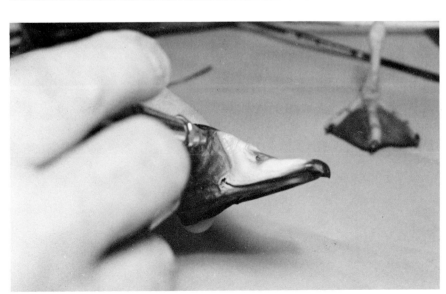

The first true color to be applied with the airbrush is yellow, at the base of the bill and at the end of the upper mandible, but not on the nail.

The Mannikin Companion Photo Series *pictures the underside of the mandible. Each photograph is enclosed in plastic, and the pictures lie flat. The album costs about fifteen dollars.*

These mannikin companion albums also have color pictures of feet. The artificial feet should be painted with an airbrush. Start with a basecoat of orangish yellow. The knuckles should have a darker value of orange-yellow. Black can be added to darken the mix.

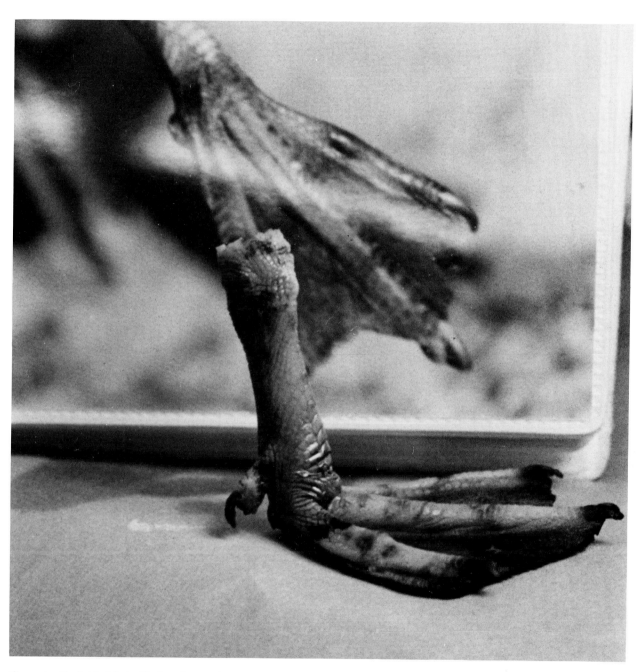

Comparing the finished foot with the reference photo.

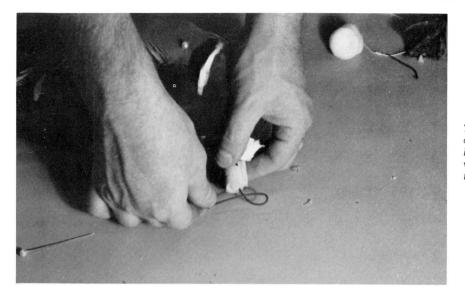

The next step is to attach the artificial head or skull to the neck. The neck wire must be looped over very near the end of the neck with the excess cut away. This loop will be inserted into the back of the skull.

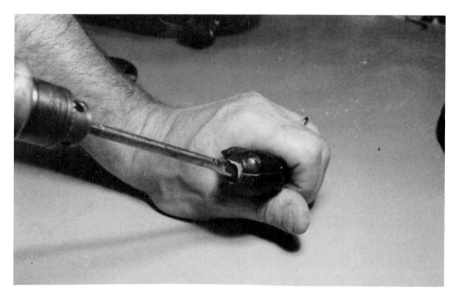

The back of the skull must be bored to accept the neck wire loop. Use a one-half-inch space bit.

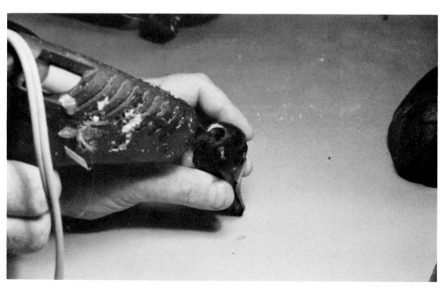

The back of the skull is filled three-quarters full with hot melt glue. This glue will allow the wire to float in place until the glue sets up. It will also remain a bit flexible in case you discover later on that the head is not positioned correctly. If you filled the entire head with glue, some of it would spill on the feathers when the loop was inserted.

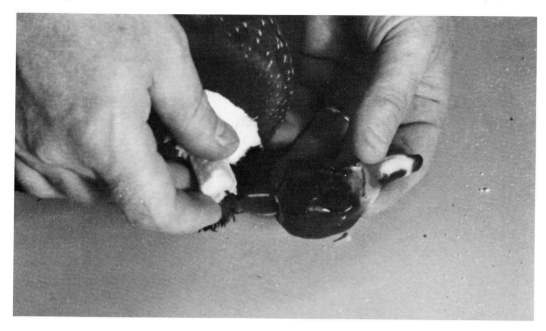

Push the loop into the back of the skull, and let the glue set up.

Because of the way the artificial neck is designed, there will be a gap between the head and the neck. A good way to fill the gap is with a water-based clay. Frank says that the clay "creates a marriage between head and neck."

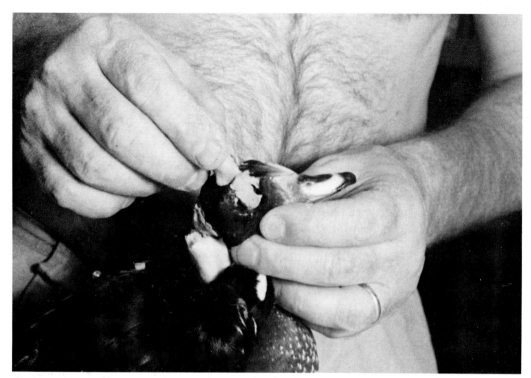

A bed of clay is pressed into the eyeholes of the mannikin skull for the glass eyes. Frank recommends using a ten-millimeter eye for the wood duck. The beds must be applied before the skin is pulled over the artificial skull so that the clay does not get stuck on the feathers.

After the clay is pressed into place and smoothed flat, the head skin is pulled up over the skull. A pin can help with the adjustment of the skin. Care should be taken that the skin does not get torn.

Next, grab the bill and move the head into the position you want it. The wire that is embedded in the somewhat flexible hot melt glue will not come loose, and you will find that the head moves fairly easily.

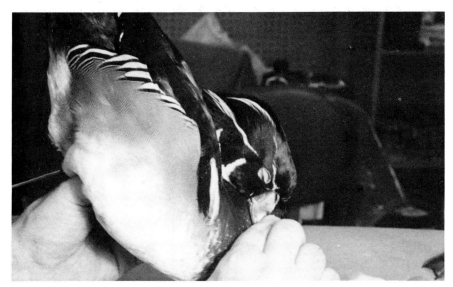

You might want the head to lie low on the breast, as in this photo.

You can position the head low or high with respect to the body, but you must do so by holding the bill.

There are two lock points on the Newmyer cast skull, both by the ear openings. If you position the ear holes of the skin over these lock points, you have what Frank describes as automatic symmetry.

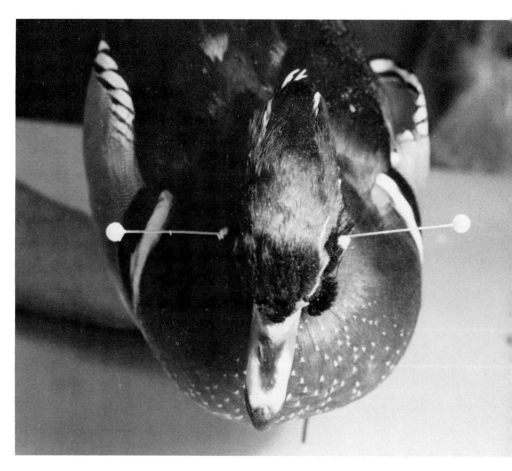

In this photo, you can see the pins in place.

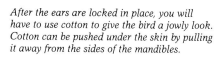

After the ears are locked in place, you will have to use cotton to give the bird a jowly look. Cotton can be pushed under the skin by pulling it away from the sides of the mandibles.

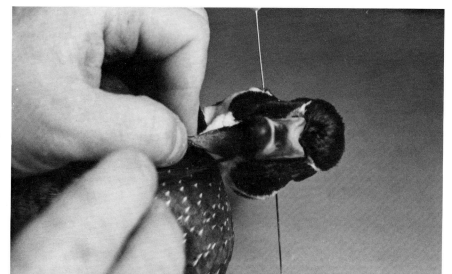

You can also insert cotton by pulling skin away from under the bill.

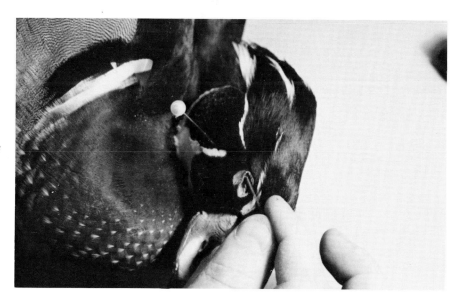

A later step: gluing the skin around the bill with Super Glue. If you do that and need more fill, you can insert cotton through the eye openings.

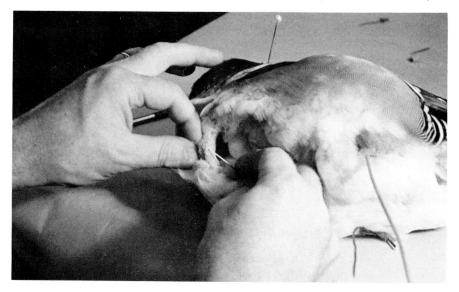

There are several ways to sew up the
original incision on the breast. They are the
baseball stitch, the casting stitch, and the
lock stitch. All three begin with a stitch and
knot. Frank uses the baseball stitch, working
the thread under, over, under, over down the
skin. A double strand of nylon thread should
be used.

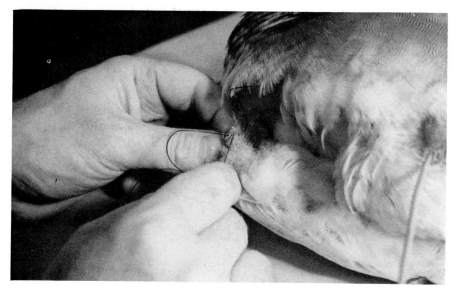

Be careful that you stitch the skin and not
the feathers. You should run the thread very
near the edge of the incision.

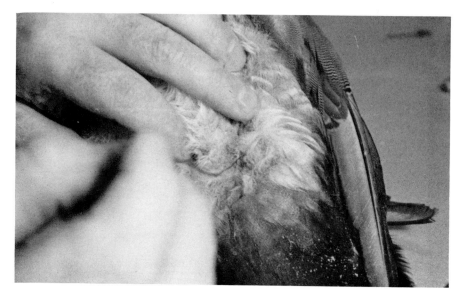

Work the thread all the way down to the
vent and tie the thread.

There will be a gap, however, between the back of the skull and the neck. This gap must be filled. A water-based clay works well, or a two-part plumber's epoxy can be used. Fingers and a modeling tool will shape the clay.

There is one more step before the skin is pulled up and locked into place, and that is making a "bed" for the glass eyes. The clay employed for the neck can be used here. The skin is not taxied into place until the bed is made to avoid getting clay on the facial feathers. Placement of the eyes is described in the next chapter.

The head and neck can now be bent into different positions by holding onto the bill. Since the neck is flexible, the head should not break away.

There are two lock points on the Newmyer cast skull, and these are located where the ear openings would be. If the ear holes in the skin are pulled over the lock points, head symmetry will be achieved. The skin is then locked in place with long pins on either side of the head.

Before the skin is permanently fixed to the skull, cotton will have to be inserted on either side of the mandibles to give the duck back its jowls.

The mount is now ready for sewing. Frank recommends sewing the skin from the top of the breast to the vent, using a three-corner needle and light nylon thread. If there is any need for more cotton fill in the sides or tail section, now is the time to put it in. The taxidermist must be careful as he sews to make sure that no feathers are caught within the stitches. Using a baseball stitch, he should keep the stitches about one quarter inch apart. As the sewing progresses the plumage should lie correctly along the incision, and any cotton fill that may be poking out of the seam can be pushed back into the skin. When the stitching is complete, the thread is tied off. If a neck incision had to be made to remove the skull, this, too, will have to be sewn up.

Once the incisions are sewn, the bird can be attached to the base. The feet should have been painted by this time, and they can be pushed up onto the two wires that protrude from the bottom of the duck. Frank's artificial feet have predrilled holes, so insertion should be fairly easy. The feet are pushed up the wires until they butt against the tibia bones.

Enough wire should be left over so that the ends can be pushed through the rock and bent over on the bottom. They are then stapled in place.

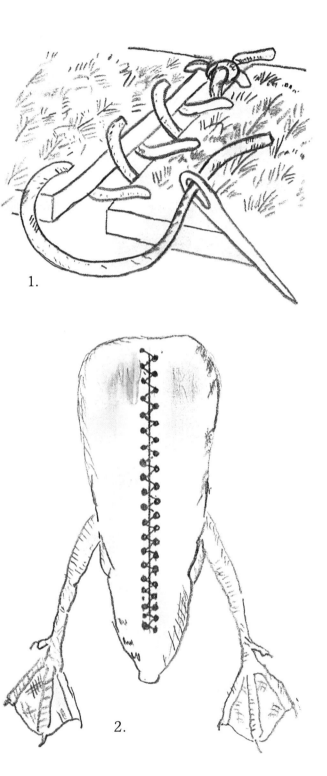

1.

2.

No. 1. The baseball stitch Frank uses to close up the skin incision.

No. 2. The stitching of the ventral incision.

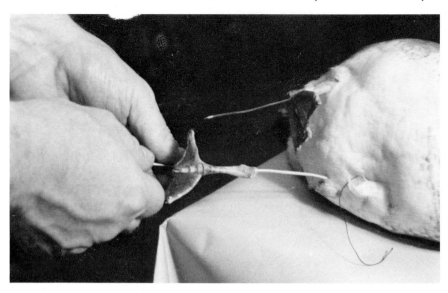

You should have two good lengths of wire protruding from the bottom of the duck for the feet. Frank's cast feet are predrilled for a fourteen-gauge wire. If the wire is too big, the holes can be enlarged with a drill.

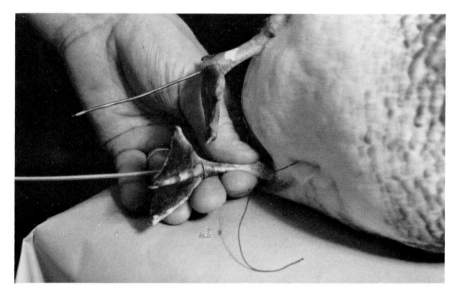

Push the feet up the wires until they butt against the tibia bones. The base of each cast foot should be slightly buried in the belly feathers.

The next step is to get the bird mounted on a rigid foam Newmyer rock. The mounting holes can be oversized, since the wires will be bent over on the bottom of the rock.

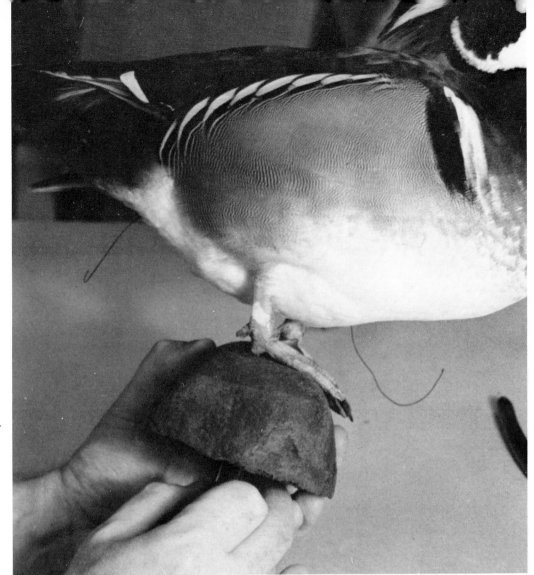

Bring the feet down flush with the surface of the rock. They should be positioned slightly toward each other.

The feet can be bent with a paint-stripping or heat gun to conform to the rock and glued in place with Super Glue. After gluing, the taxidermist should make sure that the bird is not leaning to any one side.

The next major step is to tuck in excess skin. Because of the degreasing process, the skin will have stretched to an abnormally large size. The taxidermist needs to pin the skin and tuck it in in places. He should not use string or netting, which will crush the shapes of the feather groups or flatten them out.

Now the head skin can be glued in place. Frank suggests an instant bonding agent like Super Glue to hold the skin to the bill. The two V-shaped flaps on the upper and lower mandibles and the skin on the sides of the bill must all be glued. It is best to start with the top of the head by pulling the skin flap down into the notch at the top of the bill. A pin can be used to hold the skin in place until the glue sets up. A dental tool with a pick at its end helps taxi the skin into place.

More adjusting of the head and neck can be done once the glue has set. Also, after the glue has dried, the airbrush can be used to blow gently on the bird and remove any remaining borax or sawdust from the feathers.

The body and wing feathers will have gotten disarranged during these steps, so they will have to be groomed. A cosmetic brush works well, and a long pin will help to layer the feathers the way they belong. The taxidermist must also check for wing symmetry, looking at how the wings lie with respect to the side pockets and scapulars.

Once the plumage has been groomed, the bird must be left to dry, but the taxidermist must watch the mounted bird daily as it dries so he can easily make corrections on the plumage. Quite often feathers pull away and alter the look as the skin dries and shrinks. But with close inspection and corrections, this should not be a problem.

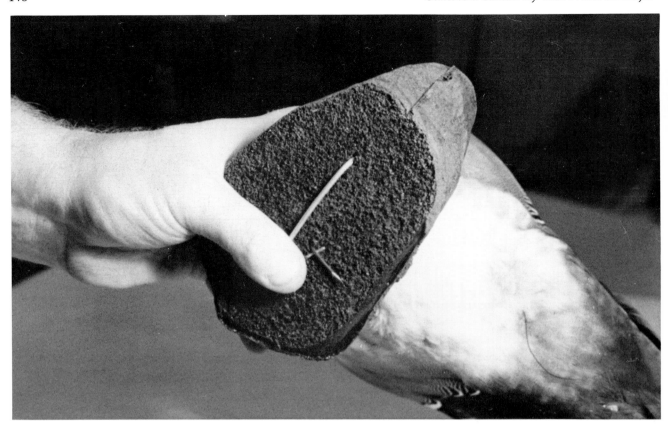

Bend the wire over completely on the bottom of the rock.

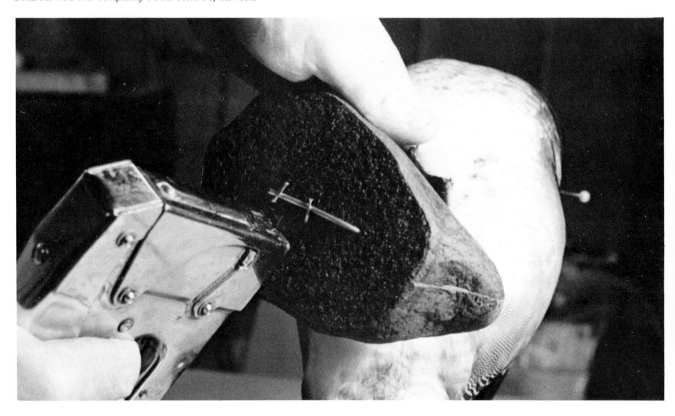

One advantage of a Newmyer rock is that it can be stapled.

The feet, although bent in a previous step to conform to the rock, may need some more adjusting. A paint stripping gun can be used to take the rigidity out of the feet. They can then be reshaped with your fingers.

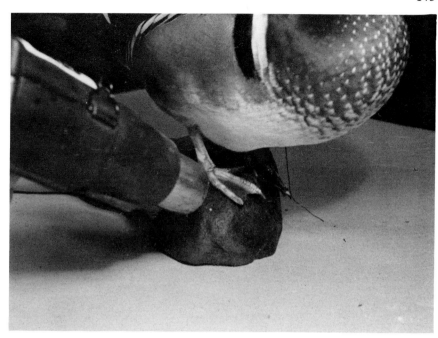

If there are gaps, Super Glue will fasten the bottom of the feet to the rock.

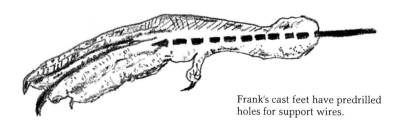

Frank's cast feet have predrilled holes for support wires.

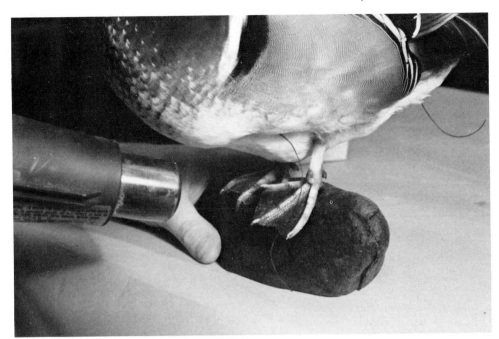

Heating the rock again will help bond the Super Glue to the rock and feet.

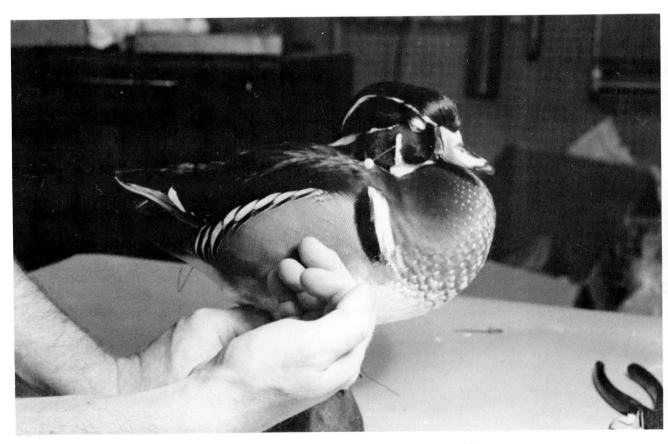

This is a good time to check the position of the bird on the base. Make sure it is not leaning over to any side.

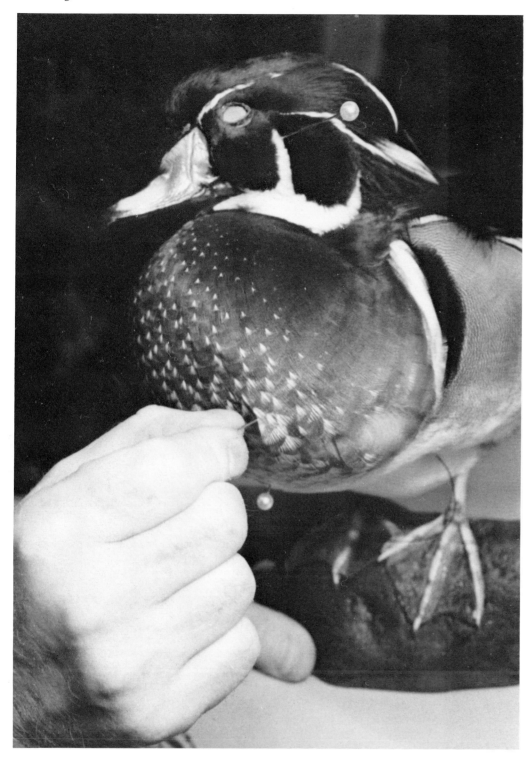

Frank says that when a bird is skinned and the skin is degreased, the skin grows from football size to pillow-case size. Where it is too big, it can be bunched and pinned. But you must be careful not to disturb the feather patterns. The skin will contract after only a couple of days, and the pins can then be removed. A cast bird will hold the pins better than a wrapped excelsior body.

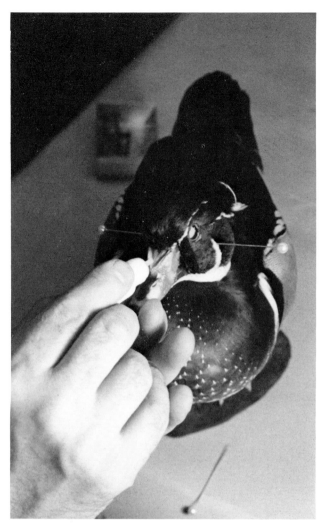

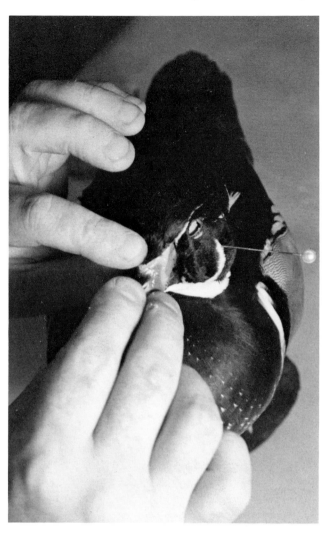

The skin around the bill will have to be glued in place. Frank recommends Super Glue Gel because it does not set up so quickly. He suggests applying the glue to the cast head, not the skin, to make for a better bond. Frank starts with the upper V flap that comes out over the top of the bill.

Press the flap in place with your fingers while you hold the bill.

The bottom V flap must be glued in place.

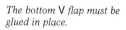

The sides must also be glued in place. If glue does get on the feathers, nail polish remover will dissolve it.

The skin in place around the bill. The pin to the right of the bill is an ear hole lock point.

The wings have probably gotten disarranged by now, so they will have to be put back in place. Make sure the primaries are crossed and pin them.

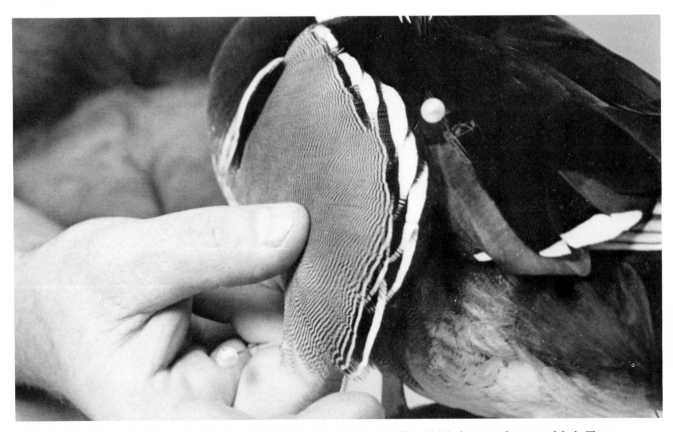

Adjust the side pockets so that they overlap the wings slightly. The last three feathers should be slightly disarranged on a wood duck. These feathers are yellow with white bars.

Feathers are stacked much like shingles on a house. A pin will hold the feathers in place or move them back into their correct positions.

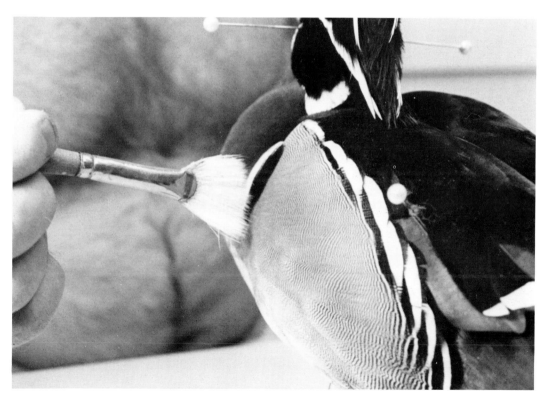

A cosmetic brush can be used to groom the feathers on the duck. Always brush toward the rear of the bird.

The pose of the mounted wood duck has been established. Note the full breast of the bird and the jowls on either side of the head. Also note how the feet are positioned and how nicely they conform to the rock.

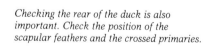

Checking the rear of the duck is also important. Check the position of the scapular feathers and the crossed primaries.

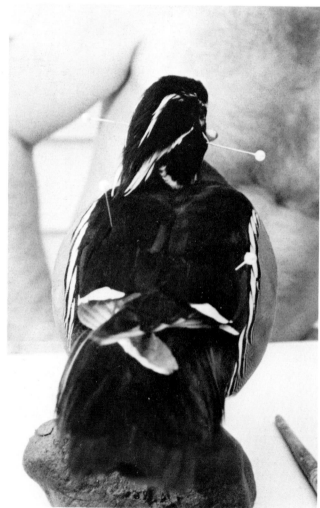

Frank has decided to highlight the inlays with a darker color than the orange-yellow mix. He uses Minwax's Jacobean stain, which has an oil base. This application should be done carefully with a brush if the feet are already attached to the bird.

In this photo you can see how the inlays have been darkened.

7

Eyes and Eyelids

Though the eyes can be preset, that is, put in place before the skin is fixed on the skull, Frank thinks that this method is really for the advanced taxidermist. He prefers setting the eyes immediately after the head skin has been put in place, before it dries.

Glass eyes will be needed. Nearly all taxidermy supply companies carry them, and most have them according to species of bird or animal. The eyes are matched for color, size, and pupil placement. They are almost always sold by the millimeter and in pairs, usually on the ends of wires. They should be cut free of the wires.

Frank advises the taxidermist not to look at a carver's chart for the size, since these eyes tend to be oversized. Instead, as a reference, he should take the real eye, inject it with water, and measure the diameter of the sclerotic ring for the size needed. The sclerotic ring is a series of bony plates, which will vary in size and shape depending on the species of bird.

The first step is to push the eyes into the clay that has been put into the eye cavities. There will be gaps around the eyes, and these must be filled in. A two-part plumber's epoxy, which is malleable for many hours before it hardens, can be used and shaped with a dental tool.

Frank points out that a bird's eye is fixed in its socket, and therefore it cannot roll the way a human's can. To compensate, a bird turns its neck. Yet a duck has both monocular and binocular vision, meaning that it can see straight ahead and side to side.

When positioning the eyes, the taxidermist must know that eyes slant down and toward the bill. They follow the shape of the skull, which is why the bird has monocular vision. A long thin wire or needle will help position the eyes.

When the bird has dried, all pins and wires protruding from the mount must be pulled free or cut away. The general appearance should be checked, and the plumage can be groomed with a cosmetic brush. The only thing left to do on the mount is to add the eyelid details.

Birds do have eyelids, upper and lower, that are folds of skin. When closing their eyes, daytime birds

Whether the taxidermist has used the original skull or a cast one, glass eyes must be used. These are available through the Wildlife Designer Series or from taxidermy supply stores and bird carving merchandisers. You will need a ten-millimeter wood duck eye. Most suppliers of glass eyes sell them according to species. Note the depressions in the face where the eyes belong.

draw up the lower lid more than the upper. But the wood duck mount will be open-eyed.

The eyelids, however, will have to be reproduced. After allowing the eyes to set overnight, Frank wraps them with four-ply string – the same used for wrapping the excelsior body – that has been saturated with Super Glue. This string must be applied to the glass, not to the skin or feathers, and the ends left hanging loose. The entire string should be saturated with Super Glue and left to dry. The glue hardens the string and allows the taxidermist to press or burn in details. Then he can take a warm burning pen or heated scalpel and burn off the excess string.

Frank points out that the string actually provides a base color of white, a good background for the paint that will be applied later. But first the indentations present in a wood duck's eye rings have to be made, using the burning pen and a blunt tip.

Once this procedure is done and the excess glue is scraped off the glass with a scalpel, the eye rings have to be painted. A small artist's brush will do the job. Frank uses a bright red oil or lacquer paint.

Next, a product called Bio-Bond, available from Wildlife Designer Series, is applied. It is a cream used by some taxidermists to prime mannikins before mounting, and it acts as an adhesive. The cream gives a fleshy look to the eye rings. It can be painted and textured, and it will dry clear.

After the Bio-Bond dries, the taxidermist should take a dental tool and press it into the indentations made by the burning pen. Doing so will make the indentations soft and fleshy looking.

More color will have to be applied, and Frank recommends using the bright red again.

The final step is to recreate the nictitating membrane, the transparent skin that is drawn across the eye from front to back to clean it. Frank says that this membrane is an important part of a reproduced eye. Its elimination leaves an unnatural shape to the eye.

To make the membrane, the taxidermist begins with burnt umber in an acrylic or lacquer paint. He uses an airbrush because it is less likely to get paint on the surrounding feathers. He must also take care not to get paint on the eye rings.

Next, a polyester resin is applied to the eyes with a small brush. After that dries, which takes less than a minute, lacquer thinner is put on the glass as a wash. A brush with bristles one-quarter-inch long is sufficient. This step loosens up the excess resin. When loose, the resin will build up in the crevices and give the wet look of the nictitating membrane while the burnt umber will give the membrane color.

After you embed the glass eyes in the clay that you previously put into the eye cavities, fill in around the eyes with a two-part epoxy compound to close any gaps and set the eyes in place. You can use a piece of wire to work the epoxy compound around the eyes. The top of each eye should project out farther than the bottom of the eye, following the contour of the skull. This configuration allows the bird to see what it is feeding on.

Notice the angle of the eye. The back of the glass eye must project out more than the front of the eye. Some adjustments can be made with a pin.

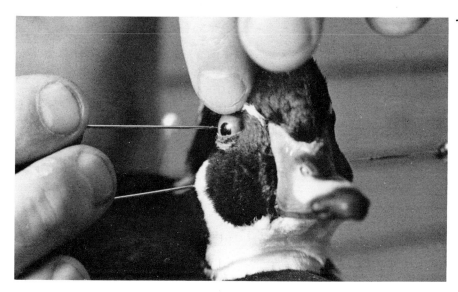

Again, the bottom of the eye must angle in more than the top of the eye. The eyelids will determine this angle, and they can be adjusted with a pin.

*Feathers around the eyes
may need to be groomed
or put back into place.
You can use a pin for that.*

*The eyes should be
cleaned at this point to
remove the epoxy. Frank uses
a short-bristled sable
brush and lacquer thinner.*

The more advanced taxidermist
might want to inject the eyes of the
bird before positioning the glass eye
replacements. Frank advises using enough
water to make the iris skin full looking.
This skin is thick enough so that the water
will not stretch it. A photo should be
taken of how the water-injected eyes look.

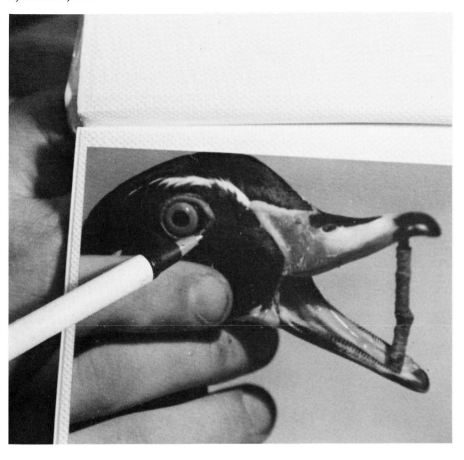

In his Mannikin Companion Photo Series *for the wood duck, Frank points to the fleshy eye ring of the bird. The upper part of the ring, he explains, is larger than the lower part. This shape can be recreated with string around the glass eyes of the mount. The eyes should, however, be allowed to set overnight before making the eye rings.*

The first step in making the eye rings is to apply Super Glue to the glass and at the edge of the skin. Care should be taken that glue does not get on the feathers.

The four-ply string that is used to wrap an excelsior body is used for the eye rings. Do not worry about the excess because it can easily be removed later on.

You can use the Mannikin Companion Photo Series *as a guide in making the eyelids.*

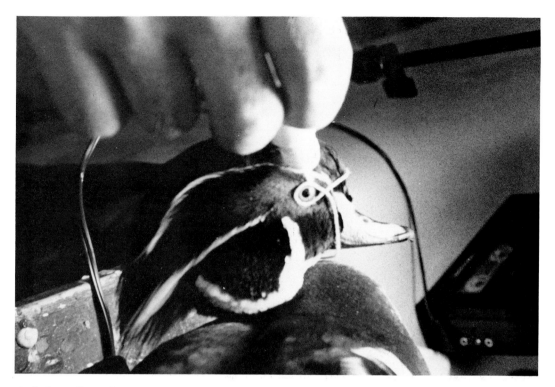

Apply Super Glue to the string. Doing so will harden it and make for a better surface when shaping and texturing it.

The excess string can be cut off with a burning pen that has a skew tip. This should be done after the Super Glue has dried, for heat may generate poisonous fumes if the glue is still wet. Be sure not to burn the feathers.

The eye rings of the wood duck have indentations, which can be burned in with the burning pen. A blunt tip is probably best for this operation.

This photo shows the indentations burned in around the eye ring.

Glue will probably have gotten on the eyes when it was applied to the string. A sharp scalpel blade will get the glue off after it has hardened.

The eye rings must next be painted. Frank will use either red oil paint or lacquer paint. Frank suggests using a size 00 artist's brush.

The next step is to build up the eye rings a bit, giving them a fleshy appearance. Frank uses Bio-Bond, which is a combination of Elmer's Glue, latex, and glycerin. It is white when wet, but it dries clear and can be applied with a small, pointy artist's brush.

After the Bio-Bond dries, take a dental tool like the one in the photograph and press it into the indentations made with the burning tool. This procedure will give the eye rings a soft, fleshy appearance.

An eye ring so far.

Some color will have to be applied again to the eye rings. Use red and apply with a pointy artist's brush.

The nictitating membrane has yet to be done. This is a transparent skin that cleans the eyeballs. It closes from the front to the back of the eyes. The first step in making it is to apply a brown umber acrylic lacquer right on the eyes with an airbrush. Make sure the paint goes on the glass and not on the eye rings.

Then a polyester resin sold by plastic supply companies is applied to the eyes with a small brush.

A brush with cut-down bristles is used to wash each eyeball with lacquer thinner. Some thinner can be wiped off on a paper towel. Excess resin will float into the crevices, leaving the look of a moist eye with the nictitating membrane. The eye should have a brown umber color to it.

The finished eye of the wood duck mount.

8

Presentation and Habitat

After the mounting and drying, it is hoped that the taxidermist will have achieved a serene-looking wood duck, one that worries about nothing but being a duck. All that is left is the habitat.

For a wood duck, Frank suggests what he describes as a "backwater presentation," a habitat with grimy, mucky water, dead limbs, and aquatic plants. This scene is not as unappealing as it may seem, for the colors and textures will complement the male wood duck's coloration. It will be no less than a piece of the wet, backwater system that the species frequents.

But what of the art? Is a mounted bird surrounded by its natural surroundings really artistic? The word art derived from two Italian Renaissance words: *arti* and *arte*. *Arti* described the craft guilds of the Middle Ages. *Arte* was the word for craftsmanship, and it suggested a knowledge of materials used by the artist. *Arte* also meant the skillful use of these materials to imitate or suggest nature. Art, as it has derived from history, encompasses both technique and interpretation.

Art also uses visual signs to convey feelings or moods. It is a language as much of experience as it is of information. Unfortunately, the feelings and moods conveyed by art are difficult to put into words. But Frank is thoroughly conscious of what he is doing with his taxidermy. Given his skillful handling and manipulation of a variety of materials, he is making statements about the natural history of wildfowl, not only by the shapes of the components but also by their positions and their colors. Some of the statements are about serenity. Others are about conflict and dramatic movement. But they are definitely there if the viewer is willing to sit back and sample Frank's work with his feelings as well as his mind.

Many carvers employ metals to make plants and wood and putty to recreate ground. Resins will recreate the look of water. Frank uses many of the same materials himself. But there is one he favors for many components of habitat, and that is foam. It can be poured to fit almost any shape; it can be molded after it is poured; and it is easy to work with if the catalyst

A severe-looking wood duck. Illustration by William Brandenburg.

and resin are mixed correctly. With foam, Frank can recreate mud banks, rocks, plants, and even wood. For him, it is extremely versatile.

To house the wood duck, Frank has styled an Executive Case which has an oak base that measures twenty-two and a half inches by twelve inches. Its corners are mitered, and there is a slot for the glass that will enclose the mount. The bottom is Masonite, which will accept a variety of paints and chemicals.

Though murky water and mud will be in the scene, there will also be some limbs to add interest and design to the overall piece. Frank collects bits of dead limbs with interesting shapes, soaks them in a bucket of bleach, and dries them. Most will turn gray, a neutral color that does not distract from the bird.

The bird and limbs will have to be moved about and arranged so that they do not overstep the glass panels. Also, the wood of the case will have to be taped off with clear tape or masking tape so that the chemicals used later will not damage the finish. But the tape must not overlap the oval opening of the case because the habitat will be built into it.

After spraying the Masonite with a flat black enamel paint, which will act as a basecoat for the brackish water, Frank places the wood duck and its cast rock into the oval and finds its best location. The piece will be locked in place by pouring foam later, though hot melt glue can be used for the time being.

The muddy bank will be made from poured foam. Frank uses a three-pound-density rigid foam. It will begin to set up within minutes, and in fifteen to twenty minutes it will be hard. The foam picks up air when poured, and this air must be removed. The taxidermist can eliminate it by pressing the foam with his fingers before it dries.

As the foam dries some shaping can be done to create an irregular bank. It should surround the rock so that the two blend together. But the taxidermist must be careful that the foam does not get on the feet of the bird.

Before the foam dries, the tree limbs chosen for design and composition are set in place. Though the foam will lock them in, hot melt glue should also be applied to secure them to the Masonite base.

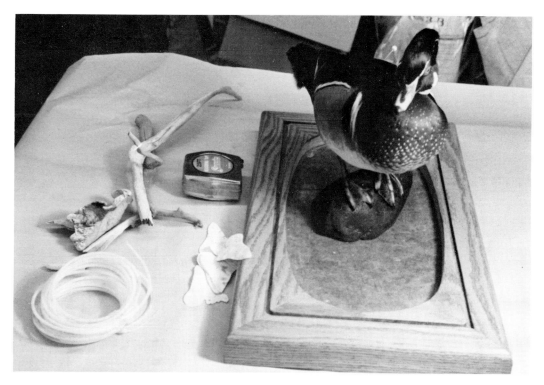

Frank has chosen a backwater scene in which to present the wood duck. Wood ducks like swampy, undisturbed water found in inaccessible areas. There may be mud, dead limbs, and aquatic plants. Some of the items Frank has gathered to recreate this scene are plastic tubing and paper leaves, which will make up plant life, and a piece of driftwood he has preserved. Frank takes limbs such as the one in the photo and soaks them in a bucket of bleach and powdered borax for a week or more. Then he dries them out for perhaps a month. The borax, he says, acts as a preservative, and the bleach not only removes the dirt but also lightens the color of the limbs. The driftwood, he says, is for line and design.

Frank positions the wood duck in the base. The glass fits into the groove.

The next step is to tape off the oak base to prevent the various chemicals and paints used later from spilling onto the finished wood. Frank says clear tape lets him still see the groove.

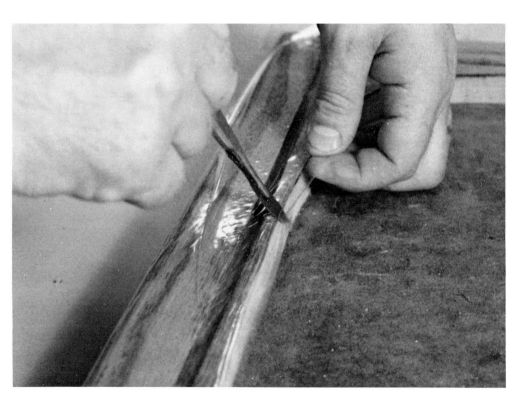

The tape must be cut and trimmed on the inside so that it does not interfere with the making of the habitat. The tape will have to be removed later on, and if it goes into the recess, removing it could pull the habitat loose.

A backwater scene is usually murky looking, so Frank gives the Masonite bottom a black basecoat. Frank suggests using a fast-drying flat black enamel.

Frank checks out different positions with the limb and determines with the tape measure that it will fit into the glass, which is fourteen inches high.

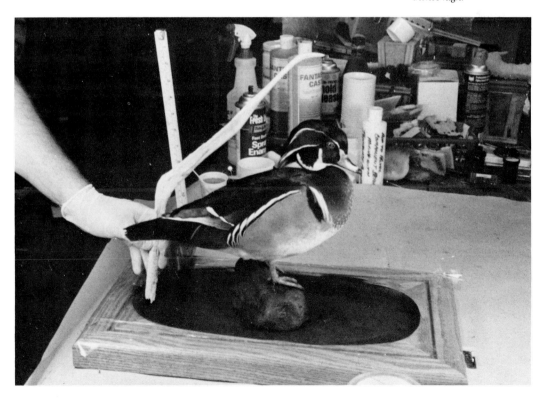

The Newmyer rock will be part of a muddy bank. To make the rest of the bank, Frank uses a three-pound-density rigid foam, available from a foam company. This is a 1:1 mixture of parts A and B. Frank says that it is better to mix too little than too much. He adds that you should start slowly and learn how the foam works and sets up.

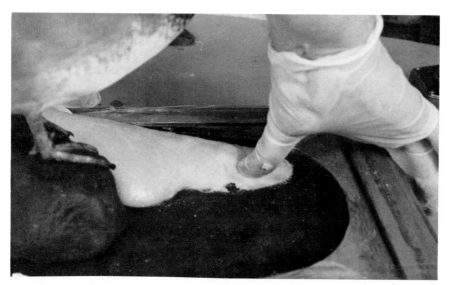

Air will be in the foam, which will affect the final shape. It must be pressed out. Timing is important here. The foam must not be set up or be too loose. Frank says it should feel spongy while not sticking to one's hands.

Here Frank presses and shapes the foam. The bird will have to be positioned correctly because the foam will lock in the rock.

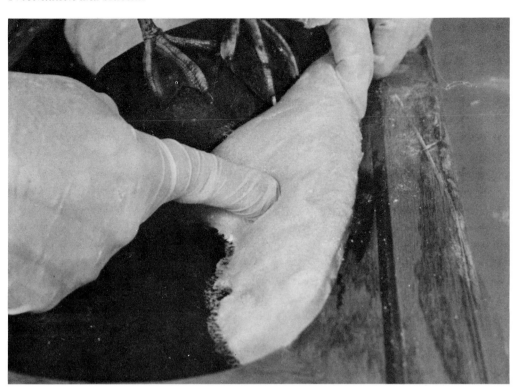

More shaping. To create interest, Frank makes indentations in the foam.

Frank presses his fingers under the foam to add to the design of the piece.

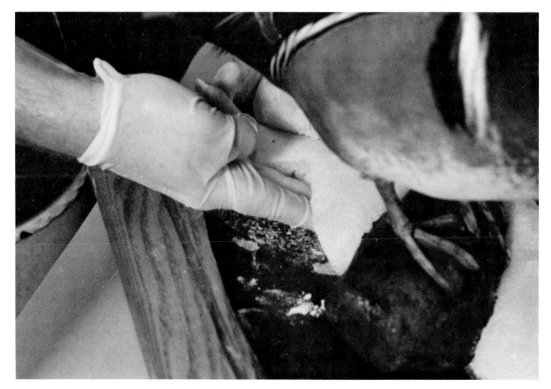

*Here you can see how
the work progresses.
The rock should be
unified with the foam.
Care should be taken
not to get foam on
the feet of the duck.
But if you do, you can
use lacquer thinner
to remove it.*

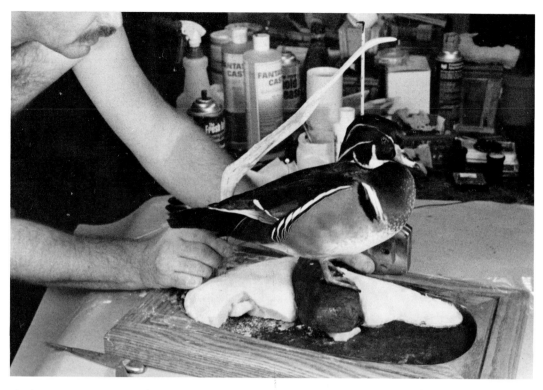

The foam will set up in ten to fifteen minutes given a temperature of seventy degrees, and Frank has cut out a small wedge of foam. He will have another limb "falling down" into that space.

Frank positions the original limb. The foam will hold it to some degree, but hot melt glue should also be applied between the Masonite and the limb. Frank has inserted another limb into the composition. The neutral colors of the limbs as well as their textures offer a pleasing contrast to the wood duck. But, he warns, there is a tendency for taxidermists to clutter their compositions, so too much wood should be avoided.

The next step is to make the mud for the scene. There are several steps involved. You can start by pouring a general-production polyester resin, which can be purchased from Wildlife Designer Series. Frank uses a tongue depressor to move the resin around.

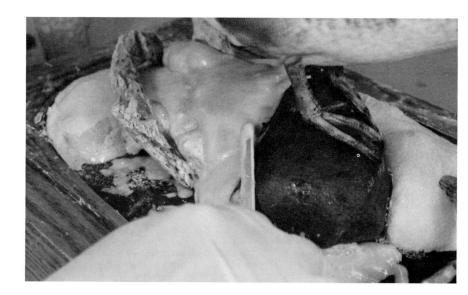

The resin must be spread so that it gives a unified look to the foam and the rock. The stick can be used to push the resin into the crevices around the rock.

Frank uses his hands to blend and shape the resin.

He does some minor shaping with a scalpel.

Using a throwaway utility brush, apply a fast-drying black enamel paint over the resin and foam. This coating will begin to give color to the backwater habitat.

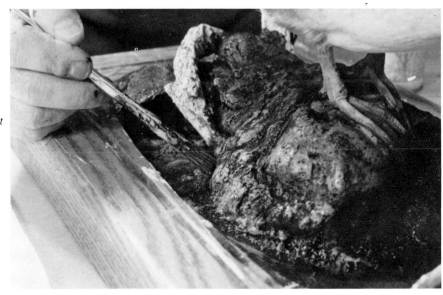

A light coating of fast-drying green enamel paint is applied over the black on the high points of the foam and resin. Frank suggests spraying the paint into a paper cup and dipping the brush into the paint.

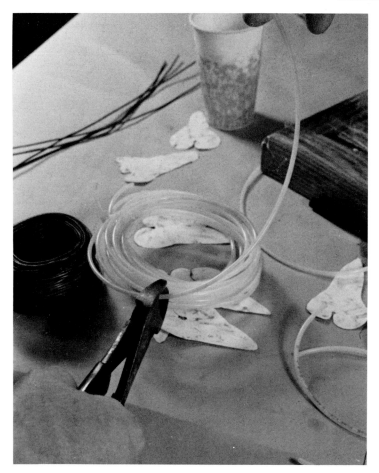

*Next come the arrowheads, which
Frank has chosen as the aquatic
plants he wants with the wood duck.
For another kind of bird he might
choose to make lily plants or mushrooms.
To make these stems he uses
a one-eighth-inch-diameter plastic
tubing, which can be purchased in
hobby stores. He cuts generous lengths
because they can be easily cut
down later.*

*You will need a light-
gauge wire that will
fit snugly into the
hollow tubing. An
eighteen-gauge wire
will probably fit.
Generous lengths of
this are cut.*

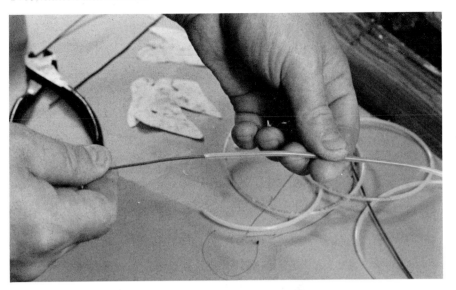

Installing the wire into the tubing stiffens it. You can bend the tubing into different shapes that will remain in place.

The arrowhead leaves come off their stems at a severe angle, so the tubing must be ground at an angle. Frank uses the side of a grinding wheel to do this.

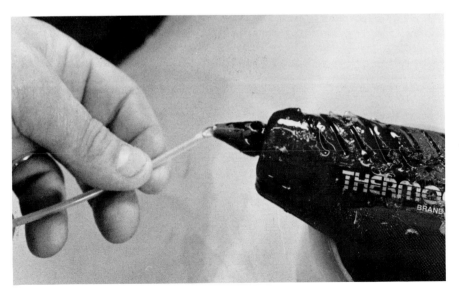

Hot melt glue is then applied to the end of the stem. Not much glue is needed.

The paper arrowhead is attached to the plastic tubing. Excess glue can be trimmed away with a hot burning pen. To simulate the leaf, use acid-free paper from an artist's supply store or white freezer paper, which has a wax coating much like that of the leaf.

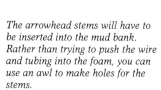

The arrowhead stems will have to be inserted into the mud bank. Rather than trying to push the wire and tubing into the foam, you can use an awl to make holes for the stems.

The stems are inserted. Frank has chosen to have them follow the anatomy of the wood duck, from tail to head, contributing to a frontal view of the composition.

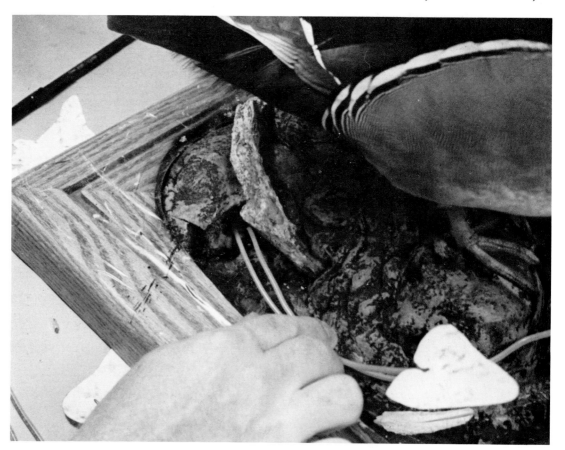

Since arrowheads grow in groups or clusters, Frank inserts another piece of wired tubing.

Several arrowheads can be inserted. They should be at different heights but not too high, or they will compete with the duck. And they must be within the area the glass will surround.

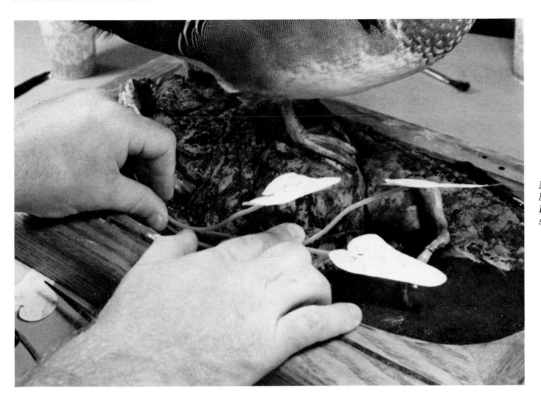

Not all arrowhead plants line up. This asymmetry, Frank points out, adds some interest.

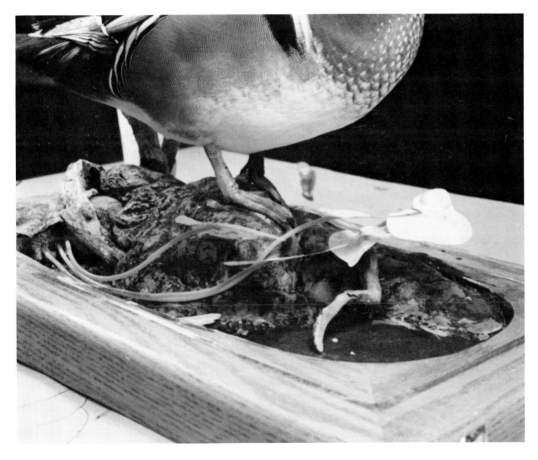

Frank has inserted more plants while giving them interesting shapes.

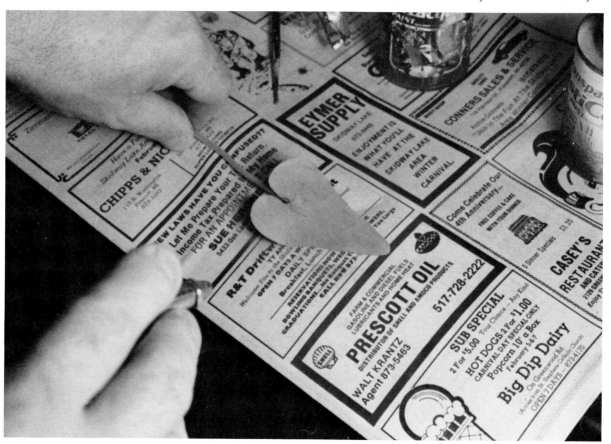

The arrowhead plants can be removed for painting and reinserted. An airbrush can be used. Frank mixes the primary colors of yellow and blue lacquer paints to make a green, which he says will be a good basecolor.

The next step is to create the mud for the scene. Frank makes his from a general-production polyester resin that can be bought from Wildlife Designer Series. The resin is moved over the foam with a brush or flat stick and will make the rock and foam look more uniform.

Once the resin is dry, it will have to be painted the dark color of the backwater scene. Black and green enamel paints do well.

Now work can begin on the aquatic plants. Frank chose arrowheads for the habitat. Sometimes called duck-potato, this plant decorates the edges of many ponds, marshes, and streams. The flowering stalk will rise out of the water as high as a foot, and the leaves are distinctly arrow shaped.

Frank uses three materials to make the arrowhead plants: paper for the leaves and wire and plastic tubing for the stems. The tubing lends itself to the soft look of the stem while the wire gives it some rigidity.

Once the wire is inserted into the tubing and the plastic ends are cut at an angle to accept the leaves, the paper arrowheads can be attached with hot melt glue.

Once the plants are reinserted into the foam, they can be moved around for better design.

The stems will have a tendency to move when the case is moved, so they will have to be fixed permanently. Super Glue will hold the plastic stems to the foam.

It is also a good idea to glue some of the stems to each other. Again, use Super Glue.

To give the green leaves some depth, you should apply some very thinned down green. An oil color would be good here. Thin the oil paint with turpentine.

For interest, you can introduce some red and burnt sienna oils to the leaf color. Again, thin the paints with turpentine. After applying the colors, go over each leaf with a dark brown oil color, such as Minwax Jacobean stain. If you want a waxier look to the leaves, use a thin application of satin-finish polyurethane.

The mud bank must still be given its wet-earth composition. Frank uses the general-production polyester resin used earlier for making the mud. But this time he mixes in debris, which can include dry leaves broken into small pieces as well as dried peat moss. A good technique for drying the peat moss is putting it into a microwave oven. The organic mix adds a good texture. If you don't have dried-out fall leaves, pieces of brown paper bags can be used as a substitute. Frank suggests mixing the resin and its catalyst in a five-ounce paper cup free of wax. The trick with the resin, he says, is not to use too much catalyst. In a three-quarters-full five-ounce paper cup, he might use two drops of catalyst. The setting-up time will, of course, depend on the climate, humidity, and temperature. If the drying is taking too much time, Frank advises using a heat gun, but don't hold it too close to the resin.

The mix of leaves, resin, and peat moss is poured over the entire bank. But care must be taken not to get it on the feathers of the bird or the feet. If this happens, you can wash it off with lacquer thinner.

The reinforced plastic stems will have to be inserted into the bank of foam and resin. Holes should be made with an awl or punch to facilitate pushing the stems in place. Arrowheads will be found growing somewhat parallel to the ground, so Frank positions them accordingly; further, if they are too erect, they will visually compete with the wood duck.

Arrowheads grow in clusters, and Frank suggests inserting four or five. But they have to be arranged within the confines of the glass case. If an Executive Case is used, the glass channel will be a good guide.

Frank points out that the arrowheads also contribute more "positive space" to the overall composition. The areas that represent recognizable and representable shapes make up this positive space or area. The unoccupied areas make up the negative space. Too much or too little negative space can give a sense of imbalance to a composition.

Frank is very conscious of balance, or the equilibrium between objects or areas. In Frank's work, this balance applies not only to negative and positive spaces but also to bird and habitat. Frank indicates that there is a danger of making too much environment for a bird. On the other hand, a piece with too many birds and too little environment does not work, either.

Balance is especially difficult to achieve with flying birds. They must look as if they are flying and not hanging like mobiles or falling down. And they must convey that strong suggestion of what flying is all about, with wing muscles expanding and contracting as power strokes are achieved.

In coloring the arrowheads, the taxidermist can remove the stems from the foam to paint them. Acrylics or lacquers will work well, especially in an airbrush. Green is the base color, but red and brown washes will add highlights to the leaf surfaces.

The arrowheads are reinserted and should be fixed to the foam with Super Glue to prevent them from coming loose when the case is moved.

The mix has been poured over the bank and into the recess, right up to the feet of the wood duck.
A disposable utility brush will get the mix into crevices.

Frank adds more debris,
which includes pieces of dried
leaves and paper.

At least a day should go by for the resin to dry. Then Frank pours a clear epoxy into the recess to simulate the water. He points out that there will be air bubbles in the epoxy that should be removed. A heat gun can remove them. Heating up the epoxy before it has dried will thin the epoxy and force the air bubbles to the surface, where they will be released.

The base may have to be tilted to move the chemicals around. You can even get some of the epoxy up on the bank, which brings the components together. But don't let the resin run out of the recess.

There is more work to be done on the mud bank to give it the look of wet earth. Frank uses polyester resin to create this look as well as what he calls debris. The debris can consist of dry leaves, paper and peat moss. Any material mixed with the resin has to be dry because water interferes with the setting of the resin. The mix is poured into the recess of the base and over the entire bank and brushed into the crevices.

Once this has dried, Frank pours a clear epoxy into the recess to simulate water and give the mud and debris created in the previous step the look of being below the surface.

The last step is to remove the masking tape put on the wood to protect it from the chemicals. Any final grooming can be done on the wood duck, and the glass case is placed over it.

The setting described here is not the only kind of habitat the taxidermist can create. Ducks can be found in clear water, in wooded settings, in winter or fall scenes. For more ideas, see chapter 12. The Wildlife Designer Gallery should be studied as well as the color plates.

Frank strongly advises putting a mount under glass to protect it from dust and the ultraviolet rays of the sun. Even through window glass, sun will fade the feathers. The mount should also be kept away from heat sources, such as radiators and fireplaces. Strong heat can create a humidor effect, which can lift the resin off the base.

Before the epoxy dries, more debris can be added to the so-called water.

Remove the tape before the epoxy hardens. Leaving it on the base too long will cause smudges.

If there are stains left by the tape or chemicals, lacquer thinner should be used to clean the wood.

Make sure nothing is left in the glass tracks.

While the epoxy is hardening you can take a heat gun to it. The heat will make the resin and debris look more like dry earth. Another trick is to add denatured alcohol or acetone to the general-production resin and debris before pouring it. Only half an ounce is needed. When the mix dries, Frank says, it will look dry on the bank but wet where the epoxy is poured.

Heat only the bank, and be careful, since most of these chemicals are flammable.

POSITIVE space

NEGATIVE space

Show Primaries

AFTER HOURS

Designing a pintail piece
with appropriate negative
and positive spaces.

9

References for Feet and Wings

At first sight, the leg of a bird looks much like a human leg. There would seem to be a knee, a shin, an ankle and a foot with toes. But this is not the true picture. The real thigh for a bird, be it a wren or a wood duck, is short, fat, and located under the skin and feathers, hidden from view. The femur ends at the knee joint, also buried under the side feathers. The first part that is exposed corresponds to our shin. Like ours, it is made up of two bones, though they are partly fused. So what we perhaps thought was a knee is really a bird's ankle. Also, the leg above the ankle is feathered on most birds while the rest of the leg is bare.

Most birds walk on the balls of their feet and toes. Almost all birds have four toes, three in the front and the big toe in the back. In some species the rear toe, or hallux, is functionless, but in others it is needed for getting a hold on a perch or for holding prey. For a diving duck in particular the rear toe is well developed, which helps maneuver the bird under water. Perhaps most important, birds' feet act as landing gear

and air brakes. In fact, ducks' feet can act like hydroplanes to effect a stop on water.

All this information can be learned on the living bird or on a foot that has been preserved. Frank advises using artificial feet for their indefinite longevity, but he recommends saving the real foot. With it the taxidermist can study how the toes of the webbed foot compress when swimming, how the foot cups and spreads out, how flexible the toes are, and how the feet bend.

Although the foot loses moisture almost immediately after the duck has died, it can be preserved with some simple procedures, and a few chemicals will save the foot forever. The simplest technique is to inject it with tap water using a hypodermic needle. Water is pumped into each toe at its base and center. But for more longevity, formaldehyde can be used. The solution appears to freeze the tissue and greatly slows down shrinkage, though some shrinkage will eventually occur. So formaldehyde is not a foolproof preservative.

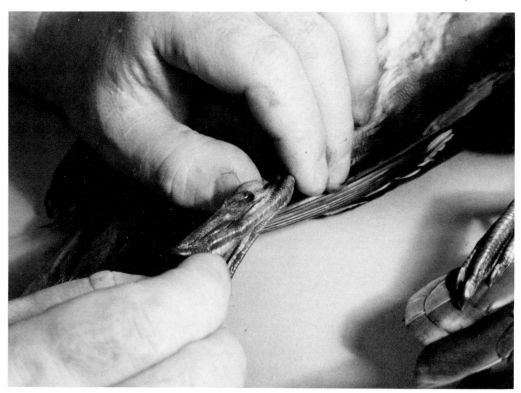

Bird feet can get very dried out, particularly waterfowl feet because there is more flesh on them than on such birds as songbirds and raptors.

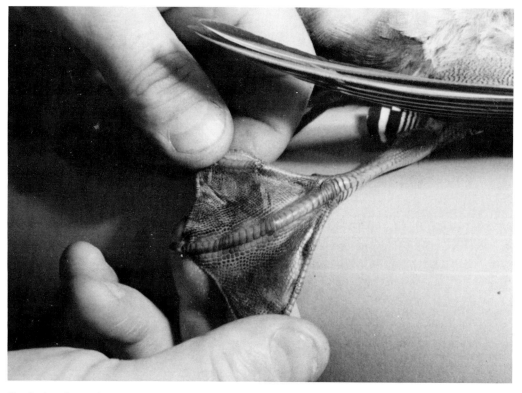

Feet begin to lose moisture as soon as death occurs. This is the foot of a wood duck that has been removed from the freezer and thawed overnight. Despite the foot's shrunken condition, details can be studied.

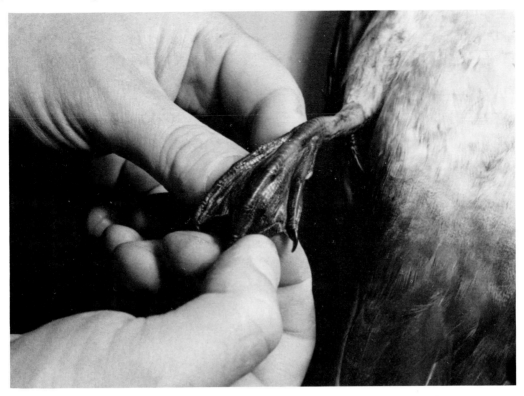

The toes of a webbed foot compress on the upstroke when swimming, which reduces resistance in the water.

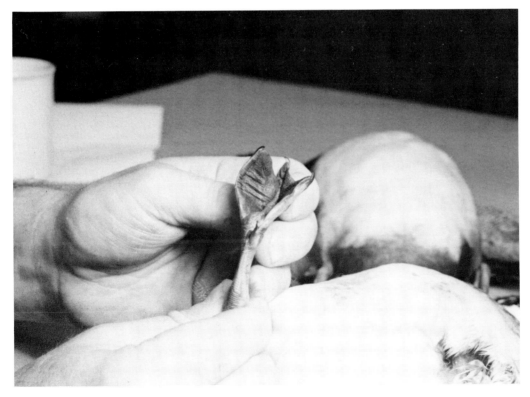

The feet can also cup, as Frank demonstrates.

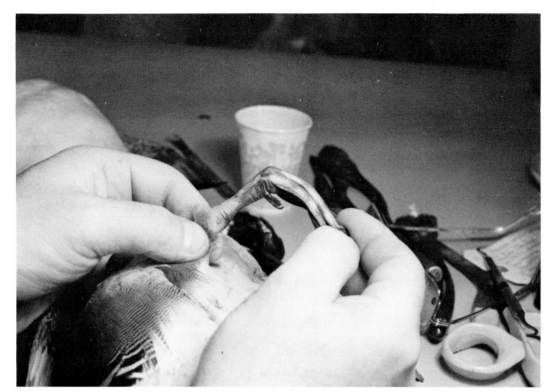

Frank shows how and where the feet bend.

Here you can see how flexible the toes are.

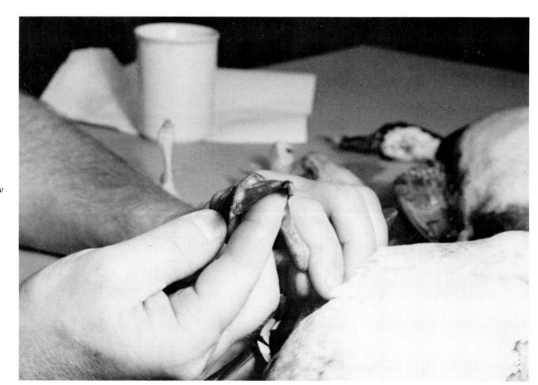

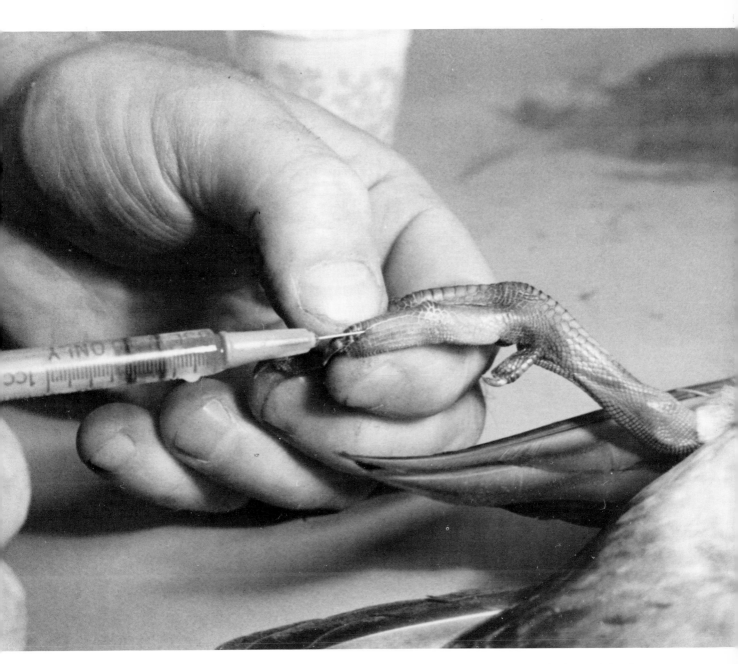

A way to help preserve the feet is to inject them before the bird is frozen with tap water using a hypodermic needle. Doing so will slow the shrinkage considerably.

Each toe must be injected at its base. The tarsus should also be injected.

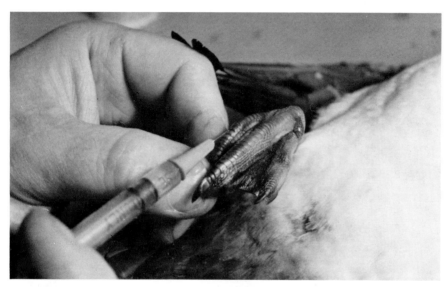

You can also inject each toe higher up along its length. But if there are too many holes, the water will squirt out.

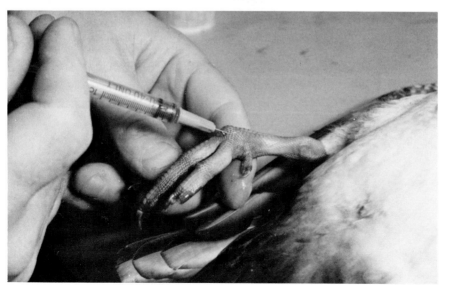

Inject the base of the tarsus as well.

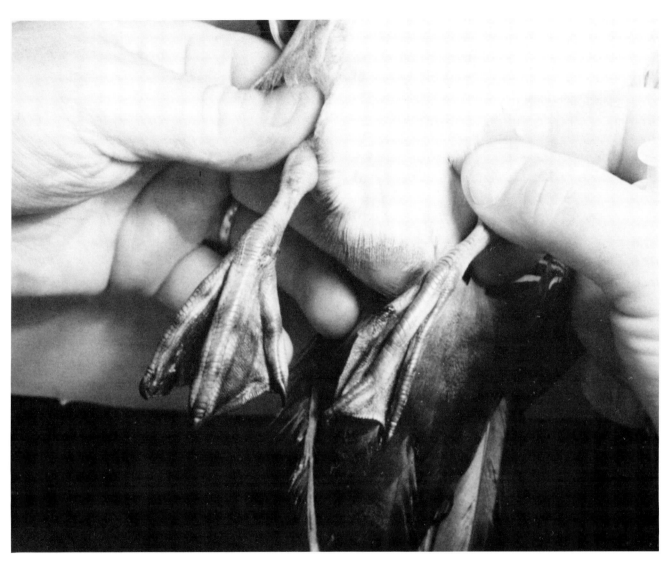

Frank compares a pumped-up foot with a foot that was not treated. Another preserving technique is to inject a mix of half Colgate glycerin and half water. Formaldehyde can also be injected into the feet, as can a product called Fantastic Cast, which is a resin capable of going through a hypodermic needle.

Real feet can be detached and saved as study aids for wildlife artists. Frank shows where to remove the foot. The feathers should be pulled away before cutting.

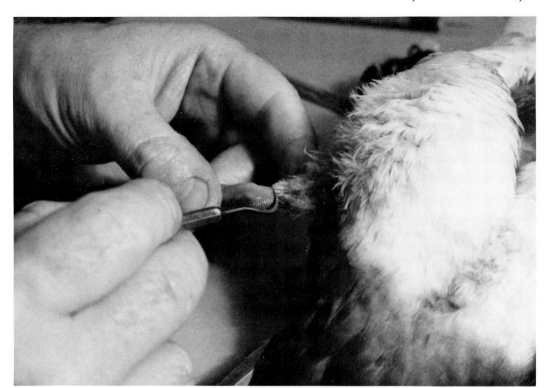

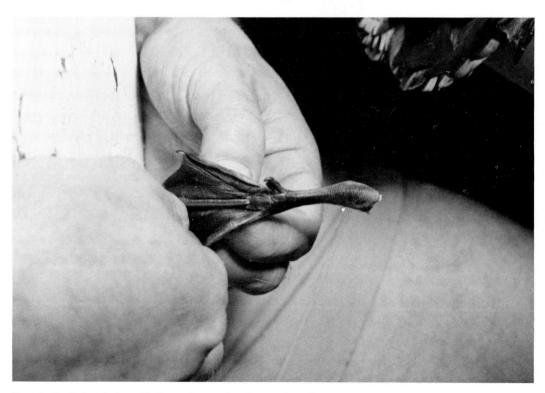

Once the foot is detached, a stiff wire can be run along but not through the center toe and into the base of the tarsus. If the end of the wire is sharpened on a grinding wheel, it will penetrate the foot more easily.

The wire should go through the center of the tarsus and out its base. Frank indicates with a dental tool that the wire has gone through the center of the tarsus.

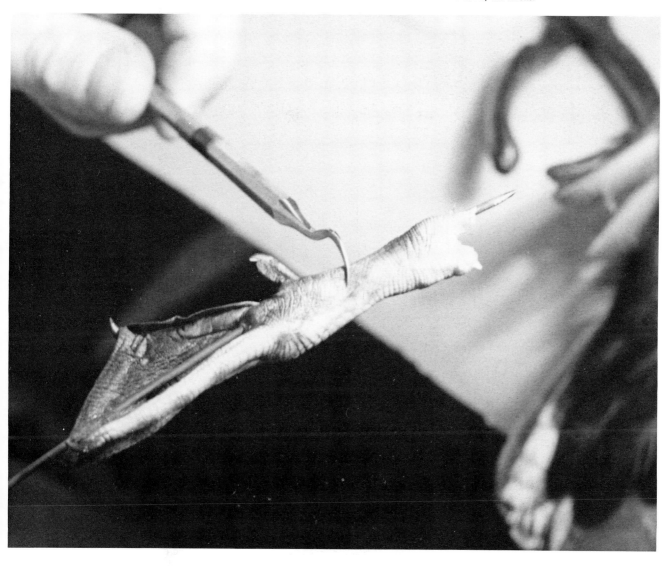

A good way to mount the foot is on a piece of heavy cardboard. You will have to push the wire through the cardboard and bend it over. Spread the toes out and pin them in place. This positioning allows you to see all the details.

A foot pinned down.

Hot melt glue will hold the bent-over wire in place. The foot can be stored in the freezer, which will also help preserve it.

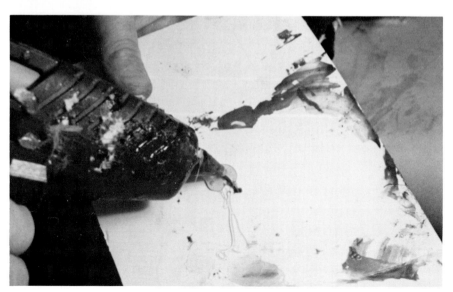

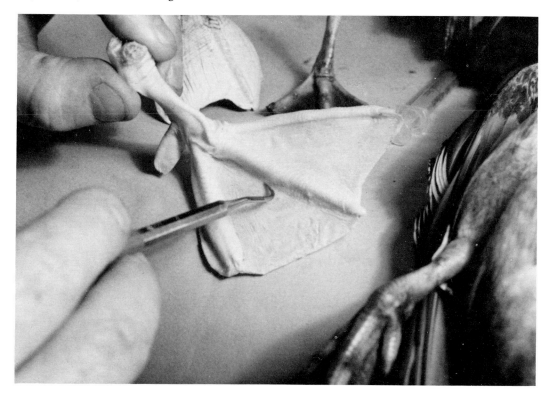

Frank shows off the cast foot of a diving duck. Note the fleshy and well-developed hind toe. He points to an area that is often neglected by carvers. Here there is definitely a transition between the webbing and toes. Frank describes it as a kind of fold or recess.

Frank indicates the slight recess on a foot he carved.

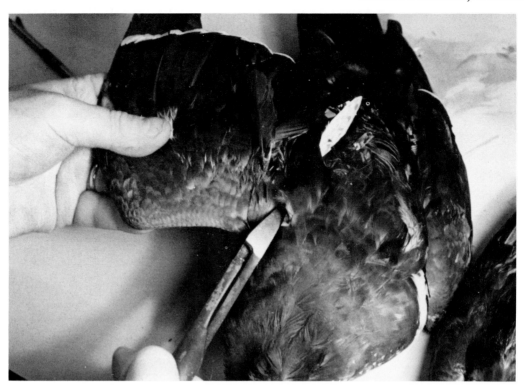

Wings can be preserved in much the same way as the feet. Take heavy-duty wire cutters and cut the wing at the base of the humerus bone.

After the flesh has been removed from the humerus, ulna, and radius, a wire can be inserted along those bones.

The wing should be injected with formaldehyde in three places to keep moths and other insects away. One place is at the digits, which are located at the end of the wing. These are the "fingers" of the bird.

Another place is where the ulna and radius are located.

Finally, formaldehyde is injected where the humerus bone is located.

The wire that supports the wing is stapled on a piece of plywood.

The other end of the wire has one primary wrapped around it to support the wing and keep it extended.

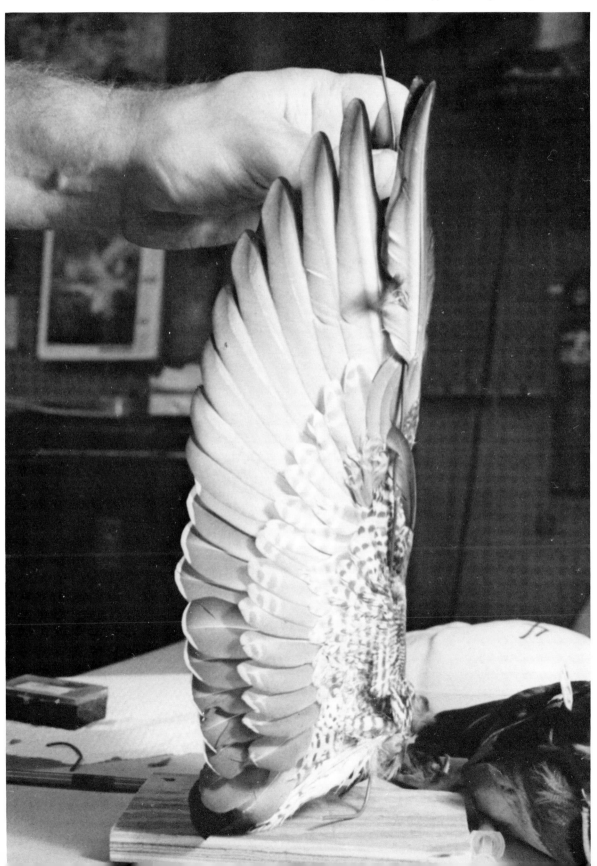

Feathers can be studied in detail.

Another trick for prolonging the life of a foot is to inject a half-and-half mix of Colgate glycerin and formaldehyde. A more permanent technique is to inject the foot with a casting resin that is thin enough to pass through the hypodermic needle. But the foot will not be flexible afterwards.

Frank has found that the best preservative is borax mixed with formaldehyde.

If the foot is to be detached and preserved, it should be cut at the end of the tibia and the base of the tarsus. A stiff, sharpened wire is run through the tarsus. It should penetrate the center of the tarsus and go out its base. The foot can then be mounted on a piece of heavy cardboard. The wire is simply pushed through the cardboard and bent over; hot melt glue will hold it in place. The toes can then be spread out and pinned.

A wing is a marvelous instrument for flight. It is both engine and airfoil and thereby superior to an aircraft, which has separate components for lift and thrust.

An airfoil might be described as a stabilizing surface that lifts a body using air currents. The shape of a wing for a bird varies according to the species. A long wing is longer than the bird's body, and a short wing is shorter than the length of a bird. But the feathers are as important as the length, for they actually alter the shape of the wing.

There are different shapes a wing can take for different types of flying. Wings can be broad, short, and cupped for quick takeoff. Shorter or broader wings with slotted primaries enable the bird to soar. This configuration is common among birds of prey and seabirds. And slotting allows each primary to act as a separate airfoil. A long or narrow shape is for high-speed flying and an arched shape for flapping, which consists of a forward and downward motion and a return stroke. Almost all birds glide with wings stiffly stretched out, though ducks do not have long glides. And there is a pointed, swept-back shape for hovering while the body is kept in a nearly vertical position.

How exactly is the wing structured to make flight possible? The shape of the wing creates low air pressure on the top as air speeds past it. If the wing is held at a slight angle to an air current, air moves faster over the upper surface than over the underside, creating reduced air pressure and the resulting lift. For more lift, the bird tilts its wings so that air moving past it increases speed. If the wing is tilted too much, however, the air will not flow smoothly, and the resulting drag will cause the bird to stall.

There is much information for a taxidermist to learn about wings, whether they be stretched out or tucked in against the body. Frank advises a taxidermist, a carver, or a flatwork artist to save a wing for permanent reference. If a bird is in too bad a condition for mounting but a wing is in decent shape, the wing can be removed at the base of the humerus bone with wire cutters.

As described in chapter 4, "Cleaning the Skin," the humerus, ulna, and radius bones will have to be cleaned for hygienic purposes. Once the bones have been cleaned and the wing skin is pulled back over the bones, a stiff wire is inserted along the humerus bone and along the ulna and radius bones into the digits.

Frank advises injecting formaldehyde into the areas of the digits, the ulna and radius bones, and the humerus bones. He recommends putting about one-half cubic centimeter of the fluid into each wing and says that he has never known it to leak out.

This wing wire can then be bent over and stapled onto a piece of plywood. The other end of the wire has one primary wrapped around it for support.

Without the wire, the wing can be used as an aid in seeing how the bones fold up when the bird is at rest and how they extend when in flight.

Regardless of how the wing is saved, an artist will be able to study in detail all the primaries, secondaries, and wing coverts.

Frank points to a definite separation
between the flight feathers and the coverts.

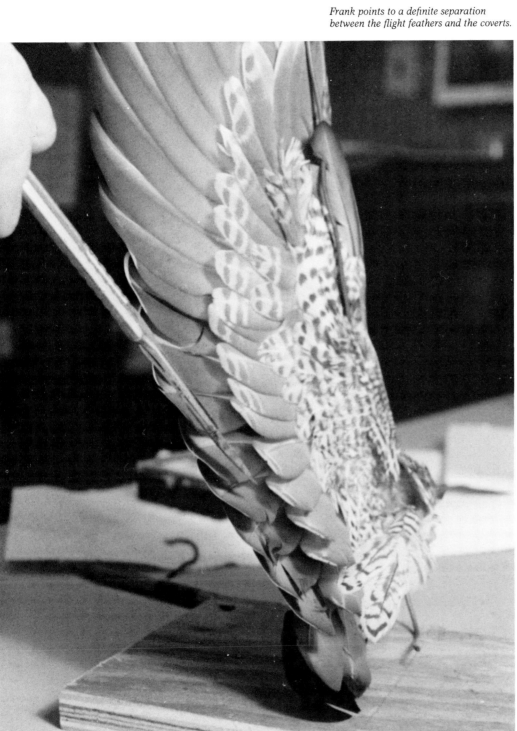

10

The Aviary

"If I've taught anyone anything, I've taught by showing a taxidermist or carver or artist the body language of the live bird," Frank says. As many as ninety percent of taxidermists, he adds, are lacking knowledge of the living bird. "This statement is not arrogance. It's competency based on my own research."

The better bird artists will do whatever they can to study the living bird. They will go to rehabilitation centers, to zoos, to banding stations. These people are in the minority. And fewer still will have their own aviaries.

An aviary is an enclosure that allows a bird to be itself, within limits. It is a place for the bird to eat, sleep, fly to a limited extent, and breed, though not all birds will mate easily in captivity.

Frank has three aviaries. One is for his waterfowl and gamebirds, another for a peacock, a pheasant, and grouse, and the third for other gamebirds that come into his possession.

Frank's waterfowl and gamebird aviary is adjacent to his workshop. From one of the windows he can see all the activity that goes on. Describing the aviary as a place where he can relax, he says he is able to watch such activities as eating, preening, swimming. Frank even takes photographs and videotapes in his aviary. He says, simply, that he is excited by all bird activity available to him in the enclosure.

Can anyone build his own aviary? Frank believes the answer is yes, and that doing so will improve taxidermy, carving, or painting considerably.

But not all families of birds can be kept. All raptors require years of special training and a host of permits. Songbirds cannot be legally kept, and shorebirds need special permits. A permit can be obtained for migratory wildfowl, however. For more information, write to Director, Bureau of Sports Fisheries and Wildlife, Washington, D.C. 20240. In some states, fish and wildlife or natural resource departments can be writ-

A partial view of Frank's aviary. The pond is in the middle of the photo.

ten to for required permits. The following are the addresses of offices of the U.S. Department of the Interior Fish & Wildlife Service:

P.O. Box 129
Newtown Branch
Boston, Mass. 02258

P.O. Box 329
Albuquerque, N.M. 87103

847 Northeast 19th Avenue St. 225
Portland, Ore. 97232

P.O. Box 45
Federal Building
Fort Snelling
Twin Cities, Minn. 55111

P.O. Box 25486
Denver, Colo. 80225

P.O. Box 92597
Anchorage, Alaska 99509

75 Spring Street SW
Atlanta, Ga. 30303

The taxidermist in particular should be aware that the penalties for selling wild migratory birds will result in a fine of up to $2,000 for each bird and/or two years in prison. Violating the Endangered Species Act, which means mounting birds like peregrine falcons without a special permit, could result in a fine of up to $20,000.

But if the taxidermist is willing to follow the laws and wants to have ducks in captivity, the aviary is ideal.

How big should an aviary be? Frank suggests that there be at least eight square feet per pair of birds. Frank's aviary measures approximately thirty by sixty feet, in which he has on the average thirty-five ducks and ten gamebirds, such as pheasants and quail.

One waterfowl-aviary owner, carver Jim Sprankle, has two aviaries, a large one where all the ducks live and a smaller one where he can isolate a few ducks for photography. He points out that a lot of ducks in one enclosure makes photographs difficult.

But the enclosure is not enough. Healthy, clean ducks can be had only if there is a source of fresh water that can be replaced. An aviary cannot function without it.

Frank and many other aviary people use a concrete pool with an inflow pipe and a drain to provide that water source, allowing the waterfowl to bathe.

To make his pool, which measures thirteen feet long by seven feet wide by three feet deep, Frank dug a hole, covered the bottom with chicken wire mesh, and had concrete poured over that. One side of the pool slopes into the water. This lets the diving ducks get in and out of the water easily, especially when conditions are slippery.

He also built in a drain for the water by fitting a PCV pipe into a hole in the concrete, which leads to the essential underground drainage system. By lifting the plastic pipe out of the hole, the water is removed quickly.

The concrete may have a tendency to crack in the winter and should be checked. It should also be scrubbed every few days.

Frank recommends changing the water every other day in summer and every third day in winter. If the

because a newly hatched duck can get through larger openings. A door can be almost any size, but it should open about a foot above the ground to keep it from being wedged shut by snow. Plywood measuring twelve to twenty inches high can be put on the fencing to prevent too much wind or snow from blowing in.

These components are important, but just as critical is the top of the aviary. There Frank advises using a nylon stretch material. Ducks will fly up, he says, and a hard wire will break their necks.

The aviary builder must beware of predators: raptors, raccoons, minks, weasels, dogs, and foxes, to name a few. Feed will attract rats. Probably the most troublesome predator is the raccoon, which can, if it gets into an aviary, kill every single bird. The way to deal with this animal is to run chicken wire from at

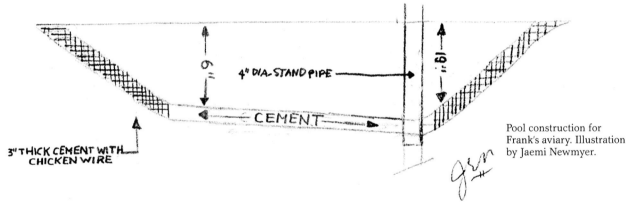

3" THICK CEMENT WITH CHICKEN WIRE

4" DIA. STAND PIPE

CEMENT

Pool construction for Frank's aviary. Illustration by Jaemi Newmyer.

water were left for some time, the ducks' oil glands would be less active and possibly not used at all. Split ends on the feathers would be more frequent, and bacteria would build up on the feet. But when the water is changed, Frank has observed, the ducks start their preening activity almost immediately.

The winter months offer special problems, and one of them is freezing. In Frank's area of Michigan, temperatures can drop to twenty below zero in February. So the water needs a heater. Frank suggests a stock tank heater that will maintain open water in the cold. The heater should be strong enough to keep the temperature of the water at forty-five degrees.

Frank points out that ducks do not like to have their feet clogged with snow. To prevent that in the winter, he puts down straw.

When building the enclosure itself, Frank recommends using steel or cedar posts five feet apart with one-inch-square fencing. The holes have to be small

least a foot up on the fencing to a depth of two feet under the ground, then at least four feet out from the aviary enclosure. Raccoons will dig under almost any fence, but they are not smart enough to go out those four feet to dig, Frank points out.

Frank's aviary also has an electric fence. It surrounds the bottom twelve inches of the outside of the pen. This fence is particularly useful for keeping predators away. But it is only strong enough to shock an unwanted animal, not kill it.

There can be health problems in the aviary that come not only with unclean water but also with droppings. The droppings can start diseases if left for any length of time. Frank advises hosing the ground every third day to wash the waste products away.

The cost for a typical aviary, say a twenty-by-thirty-foot enclosure with fence and pool, will be about $800.

Once the aviary has been built, a few shrubs can be

A mandarin duck in the aviary. Frank looks to capture such poses as this one: a bird with one foot partially tucked up in the flank.

placed inside, especially berry-producing ones that the ducks can feed on. And some strong horizontal limbs are useful, for many ducks enjoy getting up high to observe what is going on around them. Frank even envisions putting a small waterfall in his aviary, using foam with an outer coating of fiberglass. A pump system would circulate the water. These are things that will keep the average duck happy.

Ducks also need to be fed. Frank says that feed for as many as seventy ducks will cost only thirty dollars per month. He advises using a mix of wild birdseed and cracked corn. This combination is especially good for ducks in the winter because it offers a high concentration of protein. For the warm months, however, he gives them straight food pellets that have less protein. Too much protein makes the ducks hyperactive, he says. But he will add duckweed, grasses, and insects in the summer.

Ducks will eat other kinds of food: ground-up oyster shells, lettuce and vegetable scraps from the kitchen, and even insects, such as crickets.

Frank also recommends having what he calls a mucking station. Adjacent to the pool, it is an area of wet ground where feed can be put. There ducks will sift for the feed and strain it, an activity they seem to enjoy.

Where can waterfowl be purchased? Many breeders in the United States and Canada are listed in two publications: *The Gazette*, 1155 E. 4780 South, Salt Lake City, Utah 84117, and *American Pheasant and Waterfowl Society*, c/o George Searles, 115 Mt. Vernon Avenue, Patchogue, N.Y. 11772. These publications also contain articles on raising wildfowl.

The cost of buying waterfowl varies considerably. Wood ducks average thirty to forty-five dollars, with pintails running slightly higher. A bird like a bufflehead that does not willingly propagate in captivity may cost $500. Canvasbacks seem to run between these extremes at some $200 per pair.

Usually only a trained eye can tell if a bird is dying when purchased, but Frank suggests looking for dull eyes and emaciation. This problem is rare, Frank says, with reputable breeders.

There are other issues to be aware of. Michigan, for example, requires a state possession permit for which it charges a small fee. Each state has different laws, but most states require these permits. And a state may send an officer to check on the aviary conditions as often as once a year. Also, after buying a bird from a breeder, a permit paper must be obtained from a state's department of natural resources.

Despite the expense, the hazards, and the legal requirements, Frank says that raising live birds brings him a step closer to wildlife, particularly given his busy schedule. He can study their characteristics and their habits even while he is working. It is a bonus that comes with his work, he adds.

*A green-winged teal.
Frank will study how a
bird positions its feet
when standing.*

*Another view of a
green-winged teal.*

*A study of how a duck balances
itself on one foot.*

A pose in water.

A pintail with what Frank describes as an intermediate neck posture. Also note the fluffed-up feathers.

Looking at an aviary bird and envisioning its internal body.

A Baikal teal.

A pintail hears something and uses its monocular vision to locate the origin of the sound.

11

Taxidermy for Wildfowl Artists

There is no doubt that reference is vital for those imitating wildlife using wood, paint, bronze, foam, or any other material. The following are comments from three well-known wildfowl carvers: Howard Nixon and Bob Perrish of Michigan and Pat Godin of Ontario, Canada. The number of ribbons these men have taken at major wildfowl competitions is staggering, and Pat Godin is a three-time Best-in-World winner at the World Championship Wildfowl Carving Competition. All three carvers have used Frank Newmyer's mounted birds as reference.

I have used Frank's taxidermy mounts for my carvings since 1982, having started carving the previous year. I took my first carving class in 1982, and the mount we worked from was a Newmyer goldeneye. It was a very good mount. My carved waterfowl based on that mount won best in show, novice class, in the first competition I entered. That was in Sacramento, California, in 1982. Since then, I've been using Frank's mounts for all of my work, and I have done very well in the competitions.

Other winning birds based on Frank's mounts are a bufflehead that took ten blue ribbons, one at every show I entered, and a ruddy duck that won a first place at the World Championship Wildfowl Carving Competition, plus eight additional blue ribbons.

At the 1987 World competition, I purchased a mandarin duck mount from Frank. I spent the winter of 1987 and 1988 carving this bird. At the 1988 World show it took first in specie and best goose and confidence duck. It won twenty blue ribbons in 1988, including four best in shows. Without Frank's superb mount, I would not have been able to compete so successfully.

I carve full-body waterfowl with the feet, and I like to have my carvings doing something. That's another reason to have a mount that is anatomically correct in a certain posture. So I will go to Frank with sketches and pictures and explain to him what I want. And he will mount the bird.

Frank did a mount for me of a goldeneye in a courtship posture. The mount was great. That bird took a first-place ribbon at the 1987 World Championships. It also took a first place at every competition I entered it in.

I study anatomy and live birds an awful lot, but you can't make a live bird sit in one position. With a stationary mount, however, you can measure every feather, study the shapes of the feathers, and you can make patterns from the feathers.

I use a Frank Newmyer mount to the point where I

make a template for every part of the anatomy. I even make templates of the head contours, which give me rough outlines to work from. I also take slides of his birds and project these on the wall for patterns. These pictures give me ·perfect side and top views of the bird. The views are then transferred to the wood. And I teach my students to follow these procedures.

It is very important for a person to know duck anatomy before he uses a mount because there are so many poor mounts on the market. Few taxidermists are capable of doing a good enough job at mounting a duck. I think Frank Newmyer is the best taxidermist in the world. He has demonstrated that by beating all of the other taxidermists at the World championships and other competitions. His mounts are superb.

Howard Nixon

Wildfowl carving and painting have progressed to such an extreme level of superrealism that it is hard to imagine not using a mount, a study skin, or the live bird for reference, though some artists would have you believe that they get by using only a few photos.

The live bird is in itself the sole source of inspiration for any artistic interpretation of it. The time that is spent studying each species is probably the most beneficial and sometimes the least practiced thing that a carver can do if there is any real desire for improvement.

Birds are almost always in constant movement, and I tend to portray them in animated positions if they are characteristic of that species. I believe that an animated pose makes for a more interesting piece of art.

When I've been inspired and it is time to commit my ideas to a piece of wood or canvas, I'll need the reference for it in front of me. Just short of having the live bird pose for me, I'll have a bird mounted in the position I'm looking for. Still photos and study skins for cross-reference do help, but they obviously fall short of what is needed. Whatever is used, it is important to have the anatomical knowledge and technical skill to create a believable piece of art.

I've been fortunate enough to use birds mounted by Frank for reference in both my carvings and paintings. There are endless subtleties in a mount that can be found and put to use, ones that will never show up in a photo. Three-dimensional reference is definitely better than even a dozen photos.

Frank doesn't just mount a bird, he puts life back into it. He shows so much compassion and dedication toward his work, and the birds as well, that he has taken an industry of preservation and transformed it into an art form that others will emulate for a long time.

Bob Perrish

Mounted birds and/or study skins are exceptionally valuable to carvers attempting to create a realistic rendition of a live bird. They are, in fact, indispensable to those artists subjecting their work to the scrutiny of competition judges. The most obvious uses of this reference source are in determining feather shapes and patterns in different regions of the bird. The quality and quantity of feathers vary greatly from species to species, and the information necessary to capture the obvious and more subtle characteristics of feather structure and layout is usually not available in other references, such as photographs.

With experience, the carver can also develop a feel for the textural variation of feathers throughout the bird. For example, a mounted bird will usually show the distinctive differences among the textures of the loose, ragged side feathers, the stiff scapulars, tertials, and primary flight feathers, and the hairlike head feathers.

Another important use of mounted birds is the determination of accurate color. The colors evident in photographs and lithographic reproductions in books are subject to variables and cannot be trusted to provide the true color information. From a mounted bird a baseline can be established away from which the artist can venture in creating his interpretation of the subject. For example, the carver should be encouraged to incorporate highlight and shadow to emphasize form as well as to exaggerate colors in certain areas, which will draw attention to and dramatize them.

Although a mounted bird can provide information on general size and proportions, I discourage carvers from copying the form, shape, and attitude observed in the mount regardless of its quality. After all, this reflects the taxidermist's interpretation. But if the carving is to be a work of art, it must represent the ideas, concepts, and style of its creator. The information gleaned from a mounted bird should be integrated with that of other references and observations of live birds. By doing this, the carving will reflect the carver's interpretation of his subject. Only then will the art of bird sculpture remain fresh and exciting and allow our work the continuing recognition as a valid art form.

Pat Godin

12

The Wildlife Designer Gallery

*The Frank Newmyer
Taxidermy Gallery is a
showplace for many of
Frank's mounts. Tastefully
paneled in pine on the
ceiling and upper
walls, the gallery offers
the visitor a collection of
exquisite bird compositions
and bronzes, carvings,
and wildlife paintings. It
is located on Frank's
property in Gladwin,
Michigan.*

There are two rooms, each containing birds that have been skillfully mounted by Frank.

A salmon-crested cockatoo
from the southern Moluccas. It
measures eighteen inches and has
a crest of feathers that broadens
at the tip. Frank says that this is
the most alive-looking bird in his
gallery, with "a fantastic head."

He made the tongue for this parrot
using an epoxy compound that he
pressed into the inside of the mouth.
When he closed the mandibles, the
epoxy took an impression. To
prevent the epoxy from sticking to
the upper plate, he sprinkled powdered
borax on the epoxy. He later textured
the tongue with dental tools. These
effects can also be obtained with
upland gamebirds when an open-
mouthed bird is desired. To give the
beak a chafed look, Frank sprayed
acetone on it, then brushed on Super
Glue to take off small pieces of
the beak.

The leaves for the composition were
made from paper. The moss is real.
It was preserved, dried, and
painted. The limb is secured to a
two-inch-thick oak base.

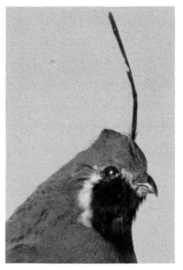

The thin head plume is distinctive on this gamebird.

A mountain quail is the largest of North American quails. Its range is from the Pacific Northwest to southern California.

Frank made the rock from foam and the cactus from Fantastic Cast, available from Wildlife Designer Series. He then bought a cactus from a local greenhouse, plucked out the spines with tweezers, and joined them to the casting with Super Glue. The soil or dirt was applied over the foam before it set up. Frank says that you can also make a reverse pour: that is, put a thin layer of soil into a saucer and pour the foam over it.

This rooster chicken won Best in World Single Bird at the 1984 World show. It is called "One Eye." All chickens descended from only four species.

A male king eider. This sea duck is rarely found in the United States, but it is common in the far north. It was taken on an Alaskan hunt.

A closeup of the head. What makes this bird distinctive is the frontal shield that extends up the forehead. It is an area that puffs up during the mating season.

The female king eider. Feet and bills were made for both male and female eider.

This is a pair of uprising, full-size blue-winged teal. Frank calls this a dramatic piece that portrays the animation of a pair of ducks taking off from water. It was carved from foam.

The heavy-looking abstract base represents water.

This duck shows the hyperextension of the primaries.

A pair of common mergansers, a large, common freshwater species of duck. Frank calls this piece a vignette. The mounts depict a female relaxing and the male in a postpreening attitude as it drops its wing down to dry it.

The female common merganser.

The female has more of a crest than the male of the species.

Frank calls this ruffed grouse
a dead-game mount. Often a
bird too damaged to
make a decent mount can
be displayed this way.
One of the problems of doing
dead-game mounts is making
them look convincing. The
birds must convey the
impression that they have been
recently killed. Frank says
this kind of composition
contributes to our heritage of
hunting, and it is particularly
popular with hunters.

A pair of pheasants
mounted as dead game.

A pair of goldeneyes.
Frank will put hunting
or fishing memorabilia
into the composition to
give a feeling of
nostalgia.

A pair of mandarin ducks. Called "The Lookout," the display depicts a fall scene. The warm colors of fall maple leaves complement the colors of the birds. The portholes below the ducks reveal lily pads on the right side. The left side is quite dark, giving a sense of depth. The birds are, then, swimming toward deeper water. This is what Frank describes as a coffee table piece. It has casters underneath.

Another view. The leaves are made from acid-free paper, and the rocks are made of rigid foam.

Frank says that these ducks, which are related to the wood duck, have just landed. They will be nervous until they have investigated their surroundings, so they do not have a very relaxed look.

A cinnamon teal taking off from water. The bird was mounted with the Newmyer mannikin, cast feet, and bill. It is "kicked over" at a slight angle to give it more animation. A clear acrylic rod supports the bird. One end was sharpened to go into the cast body, and the other end was flattened and bent over.

The surface of the water is one-eighth-inch-thick Plexiglas covered with ripples made from molded catalyzed resin. To disguise the rod, Frank made separate pieces of splash using a catalyzed resin.

A closeup of the head. Frank describes this as "a beautiful head." The fluffed-up look is hard to achieve, Frank says. Also, he used the real bill.

A closeup of a lily pad, made from thin cardboard with plastic stems.

A gadwall drake with lily pads and mushrooms. Note how one foot is partially tucked into the belly of the bird.

A closeup of the base. Frank made the mushrooms from an epoxy compound.

A pintail in a case that measures nineteen by nineteen inches. Arrowheads made from paper and plastic tubing give height to the composition and complement the direction of the pintail. The water was made of one-eighth-inch-thick Plexiglas.

A closeup of the arrowheads. To achieve the ragged, curling edges, Frank used a hot burning pen.

A closeup of the duck. To add to the realism, Frank applied a few drops of resin-water to the feathers.

This is what Frank calls a porthole. Inside can be seen lily pads.

A common eider on rocks, mounted in 1985 and placed in an Executive Case. Frank saved the real mandible of the bird, using formaldehyde and a sculpting compound.

A closeup of the head.

The rocks were made from foam, then textured and painted.

The feet for the eider are the real ones.

A closeup of the mandarin head.

A single mandarin drake in an Executive Case. The habitat is a backwater scene with mud, water, and a few plants. Frank calls this a Hollywood pose, with a "full-blown" head. The limbs were chosen to give lines of visual interest to the composition.

A canvasback in an Executive Case.

A closeup of the head.

An interesting touch is the water dripping from the bill.

He made the bill for this bird because the original was not in good shape. The feet were cast from a shoveler duck; the shoveler and pink-eared ducks are closely related. Both species of birds use the large shovel-shaped bill for sifting water.

A pink-eared duck found in Australia and mounted in an Executive Case. Frank used a muddy bank for this composition.

The teardrop topknot distinguishes this bird and the similar-looking California quail from other species.

A Gambel quail, found in the Southwest.

The "Marsh Maestro." It was given by Ducks Unlimited of the United States to Ducks Unlimited of Canada. A copy of the Ducks Unlimited logo, the mallard is three times larger than life-size. It was made from foam, with the wings and head carved separately.

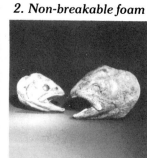

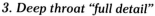

Bibliography for Wildfowl Artists

Alcorn, Gordon Dee. *Owls.* Prentice-Hall Press. 1986.

Armstrong, Robert H. *Guide to the Birds of Alaska.* Alaska Northwest Publishing Company. 1983.

Audubon, John James. *The Birds of America.* Crown Publisher. 1966.

Austin, Oliver L., and Singer, Arthur. *Birds of the World.* Golden Press. 1961.

Aymar, Gordon. *Bird Flight.* Dodd, Mead & Company.

Bahrt, Sidney, and Jex, Hope S. *A Wilderness of Birds.* Doubleday & Company.

Barber, Joel. *Wild Fowl Decoys.* Dover Publications. 1954.

Beebe, C. William. *The Bird: Its Form and Function.* Dover Publications. 1965.

Beebe, Frank L. *Hawks, Falcons, & Falconry.* Hancock House Publishers. 1976.

Bellrose, Frank C. *Ducks, Geese and Swans of North America.* Stackpole Books. 1980.

Boag, David, and Alexander, Mike. *The Atlantic Puffin.* Blandford Press. 1986.

Boulton, Rudyerd. *Traveling with the Birds.* M. A. Donahue & Company. 1960.

Boyer, Trevor, and Burton, Philip. *Vanished Eagles.* Dodd, Mead & Company. 1981.

Brown, Leslie, and Amadon, Dean. *Eagles, Hawks & Falcons of the World,* 2 vols. Country Life Books. 1968.

Bruce, David. *Bird of Jove.* Ballantine Books. 1971.

Bruun, Bertel, and Zim, Herbert S. *Birds of North America.* Golden Press. 1966.

Burk, Bruce. *Game Bird Carving.* Winchester Press. 1982.

————. *Decorative Decoy Designs: Dabbling and Whistling Ducks.* Winchester Press. 1986.

Burk, Ken, ed. *How to Attract Birds.* Ortho Books. 1983.

Burn, Barbara. *The National Audubon Society Collection Nature Series: North American Birds.* Bonanza Books. 1984.

Burton, John A., ed. *Owls of the World.* E. P. Dutton & Co. 1973.

————. *The Treasury of Birds.* Octopus Books. 1972.

Burton, Philip. *Vanishing Eagles.* Dodd, Mead & Company. 1983.

Burton, Robert. *Bird Behavior.* Alfred A. Knopf. 1985.

Burton, Robert, and Coleman, Bruce. *The Wondrous World of Birds.* Leon Amiel Publisher. 1976.

Cade, Tom J. *The Falcons of the World.* Cornell University Press. 1982.

Campbell, W. D. *Birds of Town and Village.* Country Life Books. 1965.

Campbell, Bruce, ed. *The Pictorial Encyclopedia of Birds.* Paul Hamlyn. 1967.

Casey, Peter N. *Birds of Canada.* Discovery Books. 1984.

Chinery, Michael, and Pledger, Maurice. *Garden Birds of the World.* Dodd, Mead & Company. 1983.

Clark, Neal. *Eastern Birds of Prey.* Thorndike Press. 1983.

Clement, Roland C. *The Living World of Audubon.* Grosset & Dunlop. 1974.

Coleman, Bruce. *Birds.* Crescent Books. 1978.

Coles, Charles, and Pledger, Maurice. *Game Birds.* Dodd, Mead & Company. 1985.

Colio, Quintina. *American Decoys.* Science Press. 1972.

Craighead, John J. and Frank C. *Hawks, Owls and Wildlife.* Dover Publications. 1969.

Cruickshank, Allan D. *Cruickshank's Photographs of Birds of America.* Dover Publications. 1977.

Cruickshank, Allan D. and Helen G. *1001 Questions Answered About Birds.* Dover Publications. 1976.

Cruickshank, Helen G. *The Nesting Season—The Bird Photographs of Frederick Kent Truslow.* Viking Press. 1979.

Cusa, Noel. *Tunnicliffe's Birds.* Little, Brown and Company. 1984.

Dalton, Stephen. *Caught in Motion.* Van Nostrand Reinhold. 1982.

Davison, Verne E. *Attracting Birds from the Prairies to the Atlantic.* Thomas Y. Crowell. 1967.

Dennis, John V. *A Complete Guide to Bird Feeding.* Alfred A. Knopf. 1976.

Derry, Ramsey. *The Art of Robert Bateman.* Viking Press. 1981.

Dossenbach, Hans D. *The Family Life of Birds.* McGraw-Hill Book Company. 1971.

Dougall, Robert, and Ede, Basil. *Basil Ede's Birds.* Van Nostrand Reinhold. 1981.

Duval, Paul. *The Art of Glen Loates.* Cerebrus Publishing Company. 1977.

Earnest, Adele. *The Art of the Decoy: American Bird Carvings.* Schiffer Publishing. 1982.

Earnest, Don. *Wild, Wild World of Animals: Songbirds.* Time-Life Film. 1978.

Eckert, Allan W., and Karalus, Karl F. *The Owls of North America.* Weathervane Books. 1987.

————. *The Wading Birds of North America.* Doubleday & Company. 1981.

Elman, Robert, and Osborne, Walter. *The Atlantic Flyway.* Winchester Press.

Farrand, John, Jr., ed. *The Audubon Society Master Guide to Birding,* 3 vols. Alfred A. Knopf. 1983.

Feduccia, Alan. *The Age of Birds.* Harvard University Press. 1980.

Fisher, James, and Peterson, Roger Tory. *World of Birds.* rev. ed. Crown Publishers. 1969.

Forbush, Edward H., and May, John R. *A Natural History of American Birds of Eastern and Central North America.* Bramhall House. 1955.

Gillette, John, and Mohrhardt, David. *Coat Pocket Bird Book.* Two Peninsula Press. 1984.

Gilley, Wendell H. *The Art of Bird Carving.* Hillcrest Publishers. 1972.

Gilliard, Thomas E. *Living Birds of the World.* Doubleday & Company. 1958.

Gillmor, Robert. *C. F. Tunnicliffe Sketches of Bird Life.* Watson-Guptill Publications. 1981.

Godfrey, W. Earl. *The Birds of Canada.* National Museums of Canada. 1966.

Godin, Patrick. *Championship Waterfowl Patterns.* Georgetowne. 1986.

Gooders, John. *Collins British Birds.* William Collins Sons & Company. 1982.

————. *The Great Book of Birds.* Dial Press. 1975.

Gooders, John, and Boyd, Trevor. *Ducks of North America and the Northern Hemisphere.* Facts on File Publications. 1986.

Greenway, James C., Jr. *Extinct and Vanishing Birds of the World.* Dover Publications.

Grossman, Mary Louise, and Hamlet, John. *Birds of Prey of the World.* Clarkson N. Potter. 1964.

Gullion, Gordon. *Grouse of the North Shore.* Willow Creek Press. 1984.

Halliday, Jack. *Vanishing Birds.* Holt, Rinehart and Winston. 1978.

Ham, John, and Mohrhardt, David. *Kitchen Table Bird Book.* Two Peninsula Press. 1984.

Hammond, Nicholas. *Twentieth Century Wildlife Artists.* Overlook Press. 1986.

Harrison, Colin. *A Field Guide to the Nests, Eggs and Nestlings of North American Birds.* William Collins Sons & Company. 1978.

Harrison, George H. *The Backyard Bird Watcher.* Simon and Schuster. 1979.

Harrison, Hal H. *Wood Warblers' World.* Simon and Schuster. 1984.

Heinroth, Oskar and Katharina. *The Birds.* University of Michigan Press. 1958.

Hickey, Joseph J. *A Guide to Bird Watching.* Dover Publications. 1975.

Hickman, Mae, and Guy, Maxine. *Care of the Wild Feathered and Furred.* Michael Kesund Publishing. 1973.

Hosking, Eric. *Eric Hosking's Waders.* Pelham Books. 1983.

Hosking, Eric, and Flegg, Jim. *Eric Hosking's Owls.* Pelham Books. 1983.

Hosking, Eric, and Lockley, Ronald M. *Seabirds of the World.* Facts on File Publications. 1983.

Hosking, Eric, and MacDonnell, Kevin. *Eric Hosking's Birds.* Pelham Books. 1979.

Hummel, Monte. *Arctic Wildlife.* Chartwell Books. 1984.

James, Ross. *Glen Loates' Birds of North America.* Prentice-Hall of Canada. 1979.

Jeklin, Isidor, and Waite, Donald E. *The Art of Photographing North American Birds.* Whitecap Books. 1984.

Johnsgard, Paul A. *The Plovers, Sandpipers, and Snipes of the World.* University of Nebraska Press. 1981.

————. *Grouse and Quails of North America.* University of Nebraska Press. 1973.

————. *North American Game Birds of Upland and Shoreline.* University of Nebraska Press. 1975.

Kangas, Gene and Linda. *Decoys: A North American Survey.* Hillcrest Publications. 1983.

Kastner, Joseph. *A World of Watchers.* Alfred A. Knopf. 1986.

Kress, Stephen W. *The Audubon Society Handbook for Birders.* Charles Scribner's Sons. 1981.

Lacey, John L., and McBride, Tom Moore. *The Audubon Book of Bird Carving.* McGraw-Hill Book Company. 1951.

Landsdowne, J. Fenwick. *Birds of the West Coast.* Houghton Mifflin Company. 1976.

————. *Birds of the West Coast.* Vol. 2. Houghton Mifflin Company. 1980.

Landsdowne, J. Fenwick, and Livingston, John A. *Birds of the Eastern Forest.* Houghton Mifflin Company. 1968.

————. *Birds of the Eastern Forest.* Vol. 2. Houghton Mifflin Company. 1970.

————. *Birds of the Northern Forest.* Houghton Mifflin Company. 1966.

Lank, David M. *From the Wild.* NorthWord. 1987.

Lawson, Glenn. *The Story of Lem Ward.* Schiffer Publishing. 1984.

Laycock, George. *The Birdwatcher's Bible.* Doubleday & Company. 1976.

LeMaster, Richard. *Wildlife in Wood.* Contemporary Books. 1985.

Leopold, Aldo. *A Sand County Almanac.* Oxford University Press. 1968.

Line, Les. *Audubon Society Book of Wild Birds.* Harry N. Abrams. 1976.

Line, Les, Garrett, Kimball L., and Kaufman, Kenn. *The Audubon Society Book of Water Birds.* Harry N. Abrams. 1987.

Lofgren, Lars. *Ocean Birds.* Crescent Books. 1984.

Lyttle, Richard B. *Birds of North America.* Gallery Books. 1983.

Mace, Alice E., ed. *The Birds Around Us.* Ortho Books. 1986.

Mackenzie, John P. S. *Birds of the World: Birds of Prey.* NorthWord. 1986.

Mackey, William F., Jr. *American Bird Decoys.* Schiffer Publishing. 1965.

Mansell, William, and Low, Gary. *North American Birds of Prey.* William Morrow and Company. 1980.

————. *North American Marsh Birds.* Harper & Row. 1983.

Marcham, Frederick George, ed. *Louis Agassiz Fuertes & the Singular Beauty of Birds.* Harper & Row Publishers. 1971.

Martin, Brian P. *World Birds.* Guinness Books. 1987.

Matthiessen, Peter. *The Shore Birds of North America.* Viking Press. 1967.

McKenny, Margaret. *Birds in the Garden.* The University of Minnesota Press. 1939.

Merkt, Dixon M. *Shang.* Hillcrest Publications. 1984.

Miller, Stephen M. *Early American Waterfowling: 1700's to 1930.* Winchester Press. 1987.

Mitchell, Alan. *Lambart's Birds of Shore and Estuary.* Charles Scribner's Sons. 1979.

——. *Field Guide to Birds of North America.* National Geographic Society. 1983.

——. *Stalking Birds with Color Camera.* National Geographic Society. 1961.

——. *Water, Prey and Game Birds.* National Geographic Society. 1965.

Mohrhardt, David. *Bird Reference Drawings.* David Mohrhardt, 314 N. Bluff, Berrien Springs, Mich. 49103. 1985.

——. *Bird Studies.* David Mohrhardt, 314 N. Bluff, Berrien Springs, Mich. 49103. 1986.

——. *Selected Bird Drawings.* David Mohrhardt, 314 N. Bluff, Berrien Springs, Mich. 49103. 1987.

Nice, Margaret Morse. *Studies in the Life History of the Song Sparrow.* Dover. 1937.

Patent, Dorothy Hinshaw. *Where the Bald Eagles Gather.* Clarion Books. 1984.

Pearson, T. Gilbert, ed. *Birds of America.* Garden City Publishing Company. 1936.

Peck, Robert McCracken. *A Celebration of Birds.* Walker and Company. 1982.

Perrins, Christopher. *Bird Life—An Introduction to the World of Birds.* Peerage Books. 1976.

Perrins, Christopher, and Middleton, Alex, eds. *The Encyclopedia of Birds.* Facts on File Publications. 1985.

——. *Birds—Their Life, Their Ways, Their World.* Harry N. Abrams. 1976.

Perrins, Christopher, and Middleton, L. A., eds. *All the World's Animals: Flightless Birds & Birds of Prey.* Torstar Books. 1985.

——. *All the World's Animals: Songbirds.* Torstar Books. 1985.

Peterson, Roger Tory. *A Field Guide to the Birds.* Houghton Mifflin Company. 1980.

——. *A Field Guide to Western Birds.* Houghton Mifflin Company. 1961.

Phillips, John C. *A Natural History of Ducks.* 4 vols. Dover.

Poole, Robert M., ed. *The Wonder of Birds.* National Geographic Society. 1983.

Porter, Eliot. *Birds of North America: A Personal Selection.* A&W Visual Library.

Pough, Richard H. *Audubon Water Bird Guide.* Doubleday & Company. 1951.

Ratcliffe, Derek. *The Peregrine Falcon.* Buteo Books. 1980.

Rauzon, Mark. *Birds of North America.* Bison Books. 1987.

Rayfield, Susan. *Wildlife Painting: Techniques of the Modern Masters.* Watson-Guptill Publications. 1985.

Reilly, Edgar M. *The Audubon Illustrated Handbook of American Birds.* McGraw-Hill Book Company. 1968.

Rieger, George, and Garrett, Kenneth. *Floaters and Stick-Ups.* David R. Godine Publisher. 1986.

Roedelberger, Franz A., and Groschoff, Vera I. *The Wonders of Wildlife.* Viking Press. 1963.

Savage, Candace. *Eagles of North America.* NorthWord. 1987.

——. *Wings of the North: A Gallery of Favorite Birds.* University of Minnesota Press. 1985.

Schroeder, Roger. *How to Carve Wildfowl.* Stackpole Books. 1984.

——. *How to Carve Wildfowl Book 2.* Stackpole Books. 1986.

——. *John Scheeler Bird Carver.* Stackpole Books. 1988.

Schroeder, Roger, and Guge, Robert. *Carving Miniature Wildfowl with Robert Guge.* Stackpole Books. 1988.

Schroeder, Roger, and Muehlmatt, Ernest. *Songbird Carving with Ernest Muehlmatt.* Stackpole Books. 1987.

Schroeder, Roger, and Sprankle, James D. *Waterfowl Carving with J. D. Sprankle.* Stackpole Books. 1985.

Scott, Peter. *Key to the Wildfowl of the World.* Wildfowl Trust. 1957.

——. *Observations of Wildfowl.* Cornell University Press. 1980.

Shetler, Stanwyn G. *Portraits of Nature: Paintings by Robert Bateman.* Smithsonian Institution Press. 1987.

Shortt, Michael Terence. *Wild Birds of the Americas.* Pagurian Press. 1977.

Simon, Hilda. *The Splendor of Iridescence.* Dodd, Mead & Company. 1971.

Singer, Arthur and Alan. *State Birds.* E. P. Dutton. 1986.

Small, Anne. *Masters of Decorative Bird Carving.* Winchester Press. 1981.

Snow, David, Chisholm, A. H., and Soper, M. F. *Raymond Ching: The Bird Paintings.* William Collins Sons & Company. 1978.

Spaulding, Edward S. *Quails.* MacMillan Publishing Company.

Sprankle, Jim. *Waterfowl Patterns and Painting.* Greenwing Enterprises. 1986.

Starr, George Ross, Jr. *How to Make Working Decoys.* Winchester Press. 1978.

Stefferud, Alfred, ed. *Birds in Our Lives.* Arco Publishing Company. 1970.

Stepanek, O. *Birds of Heath and Marshland.* West Book House. 1962.

Stokes, Donald W. *A Guide to the Behavior of Common Birds.* Little, Brown and Company. 1979.

Stokes, Ted, and Shackleton, Keith. *Birds of the Atlantic Ocean.* Macmillan Publishing Company. 1968.

Sutton, George Miksch. *Portraits of Mexican Birds.* University of Oklahoma Press. 1975.

Terres, John K. *The Audubon Society Encyclopedia of North American Birds.* Alfred A. Knopf. 1980.

——. *Songbirds in Your Garden.* Hawthorn Books. 1977.

Tunnicliffe, Charles. *A Sketchbook of Birds.* Holt, Rinehart and Winston. 1979.

Tyrrell, Robert. *Hummingbirds: Their Life and Behavior.* Crown Publishers. 1985.

Van Wormer, Joe. *The World of the Swan.* J. B. Lippincott Company. 1972.

Waingrow, Jeff, and Palmer, Carleton. *American Wildfowl Decoys.* E. P. Dutton. 1985.

Walsh, Harry M. *The Outlaw Gunner.* Tidewater Publishers. 1971.

Warner, Glen. *Glen Loates: A Brush With Life.* Harry N. Abrams. 1984.

Welty, Joel Carl. *The Life of Birds.* W. B. Saunders. 1975.

Wesley, David E., and Leitch, William G. *Fireside Waterfowler.* Stackpole Books. 1987.

Wetmore, Alexander, ed. *Song and Garden Birds of North America.* National Geographic Society. 1964.

Williams, Winston. *Florida's Fabulous Birds.* World Wide Publications. 1986.

———. *Florida's Fabulous Waterbirds.* World Wide Publications. 1987.

Wood, Peter. *Wild, Wild World of Animals: Birds of Field & Forest.* Time-Life Films. 1977.

Zeleny, Lawrence. *The Bluebird.* Indiana University Press. 1976.

Zim, Herbert, and Sprunt, Alexander. *Game Birds.* Western. 1961.

Magazines of interest to wildfowl artists

American Birds. 950 Third Avenue, New York, N.Y. 10022.

Birder's World. 720 E. 8th St., Holland, Mich. 49423.

Birding. American Birding Association, Inc., P.O. Box 4335, Austin, Tex. 78765.

Bird Watcher's Digest. P.O. Box 110, Marietta, Ohio 45750.

Breakthrough Magazine. P.O. Box 1320, Loganville, Ga. 30249.

Chip Chats. The National Woodcarver's Association, 7424 Miami Ave., Cincinnati, Ohio 45243.

Continental Birdlife. P.O. Box 43294, Tucson, Ariz. 85733.

Ducks Unlimited. One Waterfowl Way, Long Grove, Ill. 60047.

The Living Bird Quarterly. Laboratory of Ornithology at Cornell University, 159 Sapsucker Woods Rd., Ithaca, N.Y. 14850.

Quail Unlimited. P.O. Box 10041, Augusta, Ga. 30903

Sporting Classics. 420 East Genesee St., Syracuse, N.Y. 13202.

Taxidermy Today. 119 Gadsden St., Chester, S.C. 29706.

WildBird. P.O. Box 6040, Mission Viejo, Cal. 92690.

Wildfowl Art, Journal of the Ward Foundation. 655 S. Salisbury Blvd., Salisbury, Md. 21801.

Wildlife Art News. 11090 173rd Ave. N.W. Elk River, Minn. 55330.

Wildfowl Carving and Collecting. P.O. Box 1831, Harrisburg, Pa. 17105.